D0603407

SANJEEV KAPOOR'S

KHAZANA OF INDIAN RECIPES

SANJEEV KAPOOR'S

KHAZANA OF INDIAN RECIPES

IN ASSOCIATION WITH ALYONA KAPOOR

POPULAR PRAKASHAN

POPULAR PRAKASHAN PVT. LTD.
35-C, Pt. Madan Mohan Malaviya Marg
Tardeo, Mumbai-400 034.

© 1999, Sanjeev Kapoor

First Published January 1999
First Reprint February 1999
Second Reprint March 1999
Third Reprint June 1999
Fourth Reprint August 1999
Fifth Reprint October 1999
Sixth Reprint May 2000
Seventh Reprint September 2001
Eighth Reprint March 2002
Ninth Reprint August 2002
Tenth Reprint June 2003
Eleventh Reprint March 2004
Twelfth Reprint March 2005

(3611)

ISBN - 81-7154-872-5

PRINTED IN INDIA
By Alert Packaging House Pvt. Ltd., 326, A to Z Industrial Estate
Lower Parel, Mumbai and Published by Ramdas Bhatkal
for Popular Prakashan Pvt. Ltd.
35-C, Pt. Madan Mohan Malaviya Marg,
Tardeo, Mumbai-400 034.

FOREWORD

Cooking food is an art which comes naturally to some but there are others, like me, who have had to specially learn this delectable skill. Luckily, I have managed to understand the science behind this art which makes learning easier and quicker.

'Khana Khazana' on Zee TV has been a huge success and the innumerable letters received from loyal viewers of this programme prompted me to write this book on Indian food. This book is not merely a collection of recipes, but an attempt to encourage people to cook - and cook with confidence. Most of the recipes selected are very simple in the truest sense. They have been presented in a format that makes cooking systematic. Tips have been added in some cases to enable the reader to achieve better results and to encourage them to experiment while cooking.

While I would have loved to include in this book, every dish that one may desire to cook, obviously, space constraints meant that this was not possible. I have therefore tried to include as many of the standard and classic dishes as space would allow. Moreover, to keep the interest of the more adventurous cooks sizzlling, I have also included a number of interesting and unusual recipes. Having said so, the decision to put in or leave out a recipe has been a personal one and I must urge you to accept this arbitrary approach.

Ours has been a family of good food lovers. My father has always been the source of inspiration for all the creative work that I do with food today. His confident approach to food has inspired me from a very young age. I have always relished the unusual combinations that he keeps trying all the time. That is why, very candidly and rightly so, he says; *Beta tum to chef ho, hum to chef ke bhi baap hain*!

DEDICATION

This book is dedicated to
all the viewers of Khana Khazana
and my Family and Friends
who have been a constant support
to me at all times

ACKNOWLEDGEMENTS

Ajai Shah
Anil Bhandari
Anil Dharkar
Chef Harpal Singh Sokhi
Chef Inder Dev Boyal
Chef Rajeev Julka
Clea PR
Deepika & Vinod Sharma
Ganesh Pednekar
Gopi Kukde & his family
Hansal Mehta & Merlin Joseph
Hotel Vallerina, Khandala
J. M. Chaudhary
Jijesh Gangadharan
Khazana Restaurant, Dubai
Lalita & Hariharan
M. S. Gupta
Manoj Wagh
Mark Manuel
Meena & Ram Prabhoo
Mrs. & Mr. Kalyanpur
Neelima Acharya
Nina Murdeshwar
Rahee Dahake
Ramdas Bhatkal
Ramya Sarma
Rutika Samtani
S. K. Gupta
Sara & Vinod Nair
Satish Parab & his team
Sengupta B.
Subhash Chandra
Suresh Nair
Tanishq Consultants, New Delhi
Vijay Jindal
Vinayak Gawande
Zee Television

AUTHOR'S NOTE

All the recipes in this book have been written in a way that makes it easy to prepare even the more difficult dishes. The quantities are mentioned in teaspoons, tablespoons and cups so that the user is not scared of weights and measures mentioned in grams and litres. They have been first weighed and then converted into teaspoon/tablespoon/cup measures for the readers' benefit. These quantities have been arrived at after testing the recipes thoroughly.

All recipes serve four and the portion size of the serving takes into account the fact that the meal would be shared by a group of people. While cooking Indian food, the planned menu should have dishes from different sections, with varying colour, texture and taste.

A proper understanding of the ingredients used is vital to the art of cooking. A thumb rule to be followed is to take extra care while using certain ingredients such as salt, baking powder, red chilli powder. It may not matter much if you used two onions when the recipe required three. However, with ingredients like baking powder, any variation from the quantity stated may completely ruin the dish.

Normally, a recipe book mentions preparation time and total cooking time for each recipe. In this book we have done away with the practice deliberately as sometimes it can even become counter-productive. For instance, making a paste from ginger may take ten minutes, but these days you can even buy it off the shelf. However, actual cooking time needed has been mentioned at every stage of cooking.

A detailed glossary has been provided, at the end of the book not only on ingredients but also on some of the utensils commonly used in Indian cooking as also some of the processes. This should make life easier for the first time cooks.

MEASUREMENTS

Almonds	10-12	12 gms
Asafoetida (*hing*)	1/2 tspn	5 gms
Baking powder	1 tspn	3 gms
Black gram (*urad*), split	1 cup	220 gms
Black pepper powder	1 tspn	3 gms
Butter	1 tblspn	12 gms
Cashewnuts	10-12	7 gms
Cashewnuts paste	1 cup	140 gms
Chopped coriander leaves	1 cup	55 gms
Cloves	20	1 gms
Coriander (*dhania*) powder	1 tspn	2 gms
	1 tblspn	6 gms
Cumin (*jeera*) powder	1 tspn	2 gms
	1 tblspn	6 gms
Egg	1	63 gms
Flour (*atta*)	1 cup	115 gms
Fresh cream	1 cup	250 mls
	1 tblspn	15 mls
Garam masala powder	1 tspn	2 gms
Garlic	6-8 cloves	5 gms
Garlic paste	1 tblspn	16 gms
Ghee	1 tblspn	7 gms
Ginger	1 inch	15-20 gms
Ginger paste	1 tblspn	16 gms
Gramflour (*besan*)	1 tblspn	10 gms
Grated cheese	1 cup	75 gms
Grated coconut	1 cup	175 gms
Green chillies	10	2 4 gms
	5	11 gms
Green coriander leaves	1 cup	35 gms
Green peas (frozen)	1 cup	110 gms
Honey	1 tblspn	20 gms
Lemon juice	(1/2 lemon) large sized 1 tspn	3 gms
Mawa (*khoya*)	1 cup	200 gms
Medium sized carrot	1	60 gms
Medium sized onion	1	90 gms
Medium sized potato	1	100 gms
Medium sized tomato	1	100 gms
Mustard (*rai*) powder	1 tspn	2 gms
Oil	1 tblspn	13 mls
Pigeon Pea,split (*tur dal*)	1 cup	225 gms
Red chilli (*mirch*) powder	1 tspn	2 gms
	1 tblspn	5 gms
Refined flour (*maida*)	1 tbslpn	8 gms
	1 cup	200 gms
Rice	1 cup	200 gms
Rice flour	1 tspn	3 gms
	1 tblspn	7 gms
	1 cup	115 gms
Salt	1 tspn	6 gms
Sugar	1 tblspn	14 gms
Tamarind pulp	1 tspn	6 gms
	1 tblspn	16 gms
Turmeric (*haldi*) powder	1 tspn	2 gms
	1 tblspn	7 gms
Vinegar	1 tblspn	11 gms
White pepper	55-60	3 gms
Yogurt	1 tblspn	15 gms

CONTENTS

SOUPS AND SALADS

SNACKS

CHICKEN

GOSHT

FISH AND SEAFOOD

VEGETABLES

ACCOMPANIMENTS

RICE AND ROTIS

SWEETS

BEETROOT SALAD WITH ORANGE DRESSING

INGREDIENTS

Beetroots ....600 gms

Orange juice ....¼ cup

Salad oil ....1 tblspn

Salt ....as per taste

White pepper powder.....¼ tspn

Mustard powder ....¼ tspn

Orange rind ....½ tspn

Spring onion rings...........¼ cup

METHOD OF PREPARATION

1 Boil the beetroots. When cool, peel and dice them into half-inch cubes. Chill them.

2 Mix orange juice, oil, salt, pepper, mustard powder and orange rind in a bowl and whisk till the mixture is homogeneous.

3 Pour the dressing over the beetroot pieces and garnish with rings of spring onion.

CARROT & CORIANDER SOUP

INGREDIENTS

Carrots	650 gms	Bay leaves	2
Onion	1 medium sized	Peppercorn	1 tspn
Garlic	6-8 cloves	Water	1200 mls
Green coriander	1 packed cup	White pepper powder	½ tspn
Butter	2 tblspns	Salt	as per taste

METHOD OF PREPARATION

1 Wash, peel and roughly chop carrots. Peel and chop onion and garlic. Wash and finely chop fresh coriander leaves and reserve the stems.

2 Heat butter in a pan, add bay leaves, peppercorns, onions and garlic and fry for two minutes.

3 Add carrots, coriander stems and water and bring to a boil.

4 When the carrots are completely cooked, remove them and put in a blender to make a fine puree.

5 Reduce the stock slightly by boiling and strain.

6 Take the puree in a pan and add strained stock to reach the desired consistency. Bring to a boil again. Add white pepper powder dissolved in a little water. Add salt to taste. Stir in finely chopped fresh coriander leaves.

7 Serve piping hot.

INGREDIENTS

Chicken bones	500 gms	Oil	1 tblspn
Boneless chicken	100 gms	Cumin seeds	½ tspn
Water	1 ltr	Refined flour (*maida*)	1 ½ tblspn
Chopped garlic	1 tblspn	White pepper powder	to taste
Butter	1 tspn	Salt	as per taste

METHOD OF PREPARATION

1. Clean and wash chicken bones.
2. Clean, wash and cut chicken into very small pieces (½ cm cubes).
3. Put chicken bones in a pot; add one litre water, chopped garlic and cook till water is reduced to 600 ml. Strain and keep aside.
4. Stir fry chicken pieces in butter till tender and keep the stock aside.
5. Heat oil, add cumin seeds and refined flour, cook for a minute, stirring continuously. Then add the reduced chicken stock, chicken pieces, white pepper powder and salt.
6. Cook for some time and serve hot.

Chef's Tip : You may add half a cup of fresh cream just before serving to make it a little rich.

CHICKEN SHORBA

INGREDIENTS

Eggs 8	Crushed black peppercorn .... ½ tspn
Lettuce leaves ... a bunch (approx. 100 gms)	Vinegar ....6 tblspns
Salt ....as per taste	Mustard powder ....1 tspn
White pepper powder................ ½ tspn	Salad oil .... 2 tblspns

METHOD OF PREPARATION

1 Cook eggs in boiling water for twelve minutes. When cool, peel and place in cold water.

2 Wash the lettuce leaves in running water and keep in chilled water.

3 Cut eggs into bite-sized pieces. Tear lettuce leaves with hand and gently mix eggs with them.

4 Make a dressing by mixing salt, white pepper powder, crushed black peppercorns, vinegar, mustard powder and salad oil. Mix this gently with the prepared lettuce and eggs. Serve cold.

LETTUCE & EGG SALAD

MATAR KA SHORBA

INGREDIENTS

Green peas	500 gms	Ghee or oil	3 tblspns
Onion	1 medium sized	Cumin seeds	½ tspn
Ginger	1 two inch piece	Bay leaves	2
Garlic	8-10 cloves	Salt	as per taste
Green chillies	2	Cream	¼ cup

METHOD OF PREPARATION

1. Peel and boil the green peas. Blend in a blender to make a fine puree.

2. Peel and finely chop onion. Peel ginger and garlic and grind with green chillies to make a paste.

3. Heat ghee or oil in a pan; add cumin seeds and bayleaves, stir-fry for half a minute. Add chopped onion and sauté till onion turns light pink. Add ginger, garlic and green chilli paste. Sauté for a while.

4. Add green peas puree, cook for five minutes, stirring continuously. Add three cups of water and bring to a boil.

5. Season with salt and stir. Remove bay leaves and discard. Reduce heat and cook further for five minutes. This soup has a thick consistency, however you may make it of the consistency of your liking, by varying the quantity of water used.

6. Stir in fresh cream and serve hot, garnished with a swirl of cream.

INGREDIENTS

Fresh mushrooms ....200 gms
Onions .... 2 medium sized
Milk .... 300 mls
Bay leaves 2
Peppercorns 5-6
Cloves 4

Butter .... 2 tblspns
Refined flour (*maida*) ....1 tblspn
Fresh cream .... ¾ cup
Salt ....as per taste
White pepper powder.......... ½ tspn
Nutmeg powder .... a pinch

METHOD OF PREPARATION

1 Clean and wash the mushrooms. Slice four to five pieces. Roughly chop the remaining mushrooms.

2 Roughly chop the onions.

3 Boil the milk along with bay leaves, peppercorns and cloves. Strain and keep the milk hot.

4 In a pan heat the butter. Add chopped onions and chopped mushrooms and cook till they are soft. Add the flour and sauté till there is no raw flavour coming from flour, taking care that the flour does not get burnt.

5 Pour the milk slowly and stir continuously to avoid lumps from forming.

6 Cook for five minutes. Puree the mixture when a little cold; do not puree it to a very thin consistency. The soup should have a smooth texture.

7 Bring it to a boil, correct the consistency by adding more milk if required. Add the cream (reserving a little for garnish), salt, pepper powder and nutmeg powder. Stir well.

8 Serve hot, garnished with mushroom slices and cream.

Chef's Tip : Use raw sliced mushrooms for garnishing. However, if you wish, you may sauté them in a little butter or oil and then use.

MUSHROOM SOUP

RED PUMPKIN SOUP

INGREDIENTS

Onions ....2 medium sized

Red pumpkin (*lal bhopla*) ...600 gms

Butter ....2 tblspns

Bay leaves 2

Peppercorns 8-10

Salt ....as per taste

White pepper powder ....½ tspn

Lemon juice ....2 tspns

Fresh cream ....¼ cup

METHOD OF PREPARATION

1 Peel and slice the onions. Peel and dice the red pumpkin. Heat butter in a pan, add bay leaves and peppercorns. Add onions and sauté for a while.

2 Add diced pumpkin, sauté for half a minute. Add sufficient water and cook until soft and fully done.

3 Strain excess water, reserve the stock and puree the vegetables.

4 Now add the stock to the puree to reach the correct consistency.

5 Add salt and pepper powder and bring to a boil. Add lemon juice.

6 Serve hot, garnished with cream.

Chef's Tip : This soup can be served in small sized red pumpkins. For that, ensure that the pumpkins that you buy are no bigger than the size of a coconut.

TOMATO RASAM

INGREDIENTS

Tomatoes ....4 large sized
Red gram, split *(toor dal)*...4 tspns
Whole red chillies 3
Peppercorns 6
Cumin seeds .... ¼ tspn
Water ....5 cups
Ginger.................1 one inch piece

Salt ....as per taste
Coriander leaves..........for garnish
For tempering
Oil ....2 tblspns
Mustard seeds ....½ tspn
Asafoetida .... ¼ tspn
Curry leaves 8-10

METHOD OF PREPARATION

1 Wash and chop tomatoes. Wash and chop coriander leaves. Pick, wash and boil dal with five cups of water. Strain the water and keep. Peel and roughly chop ginger.

2 Broil and grind together red chillies, peppercorns and cumin seeds with ginger.

3 Boil the dal water kept aside again with the chopped tomatoes, ground paste, and salt; cook until tomatoes are completely mashed.

4 Now heat the oil in a small pan. Add asafoetida, mustard seeds and curry leaves; when they crackle, add it to the above liquid. Mix and heat well once again for the flavours to mingle. Serve hot, garnished with chopped coriander leaves.

Chef's Tip : Chopped garlic added at the time of tempering gives this recipe a new dimension.

Tomato Saar

TOMATO SAAR

INGREDIENTS

Grated coconut ....1 cup

Garlic ....6 cloves

Cumin seeds ....1 tspn

Green chillies 3-4

Coriander leaves .... ¼ cup

Ripe tomatoes ..... 5-6 large sized

Sugar .... 2-3 tblspns

Salt ....as per taste

Red chilli powder ....½ tspn

Ghee..............................2 tblspns

Mustard seeds ....1 tspn

Asafoetida .... a pinch

Curry leaves 8-10

METHOD OF PREPARATION

1 Make a paste of grated coconut, garlic cloves and cumin seeds. Slit green chillies into two. Chop the coriander leaves.

2 Wash, chop tomatoes roughly and add salt and red chilli powder. Transfer it to a pan and add three cups of water and bring it to a boil. Simmer for fifteen minutes and puree when it is a little cool.

3 Heat ghee in a pan and add mustard seeds, asafoetida and curry leaves. Add pureed tomatoes and slit green chillies and bring it to a boil and add sugar. Add coconut and spice paste.

4 Cook on a low heat for ten minutes. Correct seasoning.

5 Serve hot, garnished with chopped coriander leaves.

INGREDIENTS

Cauliflower	250 gms	Salt	as per taste
Carrots	2 medium sized	Honey	2 tblspns
Shelled green peas	¾ cup	Rock salt powder	½ tspn
Potatoes	2 medium sized	Fresh cream	¼ cup
Green chillies	2	Chopped coriander leaves	2 tblspns
Yogurt	1 cup		

METHOD OF PREPARATION

1 Clean and separate the cauliflower into small florets. Peel and dice the carrots into small pieces. Cook them in salted water. Refresh in cold water.

2 Boil green peas in salted water. Drain excess water. Refresh in cold water.

3 Boil, peel and dice the potatoes into small pieces. Cool them.

4 Wash green chillies and finely chop.

5 Whisk yogurt, salt, honey, rock salt powder and chopped green chillies with fresh cream.

6 Mix all the cooked vegetables with the yogurt dressing.

7 Chill and serve garnished with chopped coriander leaves.

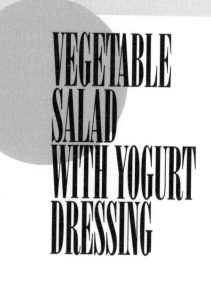

VEGETABLE SALAD WITH YOGURT DRESSING

BATATA VADA

INGREDIENTS

Potatoes .... 600 gms
Ginger .... 1 one inch piece
Garlic .... 10-12 cloves
Green chillies 4-5
Gram flour (*besan*)................. 1 ½ cups
Red chilli powder .... 1 tspn

Salt .... as per taste
Soda bi-carbonate(baking soda).... a pinch
Turmeric powder .... ¼ tspn
Chopped coriander leaves.... 2 tblspns
Oil .... to fry

METHOD OF PREPARATION

1. Boil, cool, peel and mash the potatoes and keep aside.
2. Make a paste of ginger, garlic and green chillies.
3. Prepare a thick batter of besan with water, red chilli powder, salt and soda bi-carbonate.
4. Heat a little oil. Add ginger-garlic-green chilli paste.
5. Add mashed potatoes and turmeric powder and mix well. Add chopped coriander leaves and salt to taste.
6. Let the mixture cool. When cold, form lemon sized balls.
7. Heat oil in a kadai. Dip the potato balls into the besan batter and deep fry in hot oil till light golden brown. Serve hot with chutney or sauce of your choice.

CHICKEN HAZARVI

INGREDIENTS

Chicken breasts (boneless)......8 pieces

Ginger paste..........................2 tblspns

Garlic paste............................2 tblspns

White pepper powder............... 1 tspn

Salt.................................as per taste

Cheese grated ....½ cup

Green chillies 4

Mace powder ....¼ tspn

Nutmeg powder ....¼ tspn

Chopped coriander leaves ....2 tblspns

Egg 1

Fresh cream ....¾ cup

Butter ....for basting

METHOD OF PREPARATION

1 Cut chicken breasts into two inch cubes.

2 Apply ginger paste, garlic paste, white pepper powder and salt to the chicken cubes and keep aside.

3 Mash the cheese to make it into a smooth paste. Add finely chopped green chillies, mace powder, nutmeg powder, coriander leaves and salt.

4 Add egg and mix well. Add chicken to the cheese mixture. Then add fresh cream and mix delicately.

5 Keep in the refrigerator for about two to three hours.

6 Put chicken onto the skewers and cook in a moderately hot tandoor or a pre-heated oven (200 degrees Celsius) until it is just cooked and slightly coloured.

7 Apply a little butter for basting and cook for another two minutes till chicken is fully cooked.

INGREDIENTS

Rice	1 cup	Green chillies	4
Black gram skinless (*urad dal*)	¼ cup	Soda bi-carbonate (baking soda)	½ tspn
Yogurt	¼ cup	Lemon juice	1 tblspn
Warm water	1 ½ cup	Oil	2 tblspns
Salt	as per taste	Coriander leaves	2 tblspns
Ginger	1 one inch piece		

METHOD OF PREPARATION

1. Dry roast the rice and the dal on medium heat for four to five minutes. Cool and grind into a semi-coarse powder.
2. Put the powder in a bowl. Add yogurt which should be a little sour and to this add warm water. Mix thoroughly so that no lumps are formed and the batter is of pouring consistency.
3. Add salt and let it ferment for eight to ten hours.
4. Make a paste of ginger and green chillies.
5. Once fermented, mix the ginger, green chilli paste with the batter.
6. Grease the dhokla platter or a thali. Boil water in the steamer/boiler.
7. Pour half of the batter in another vessel. In a small bowl, add one-fourth tspn soda bi-carbonate, half tspn oil and half tspn lemon juice. Add this to the batter and mix well. Repeat this for the remaining batter just before putting it in the steamer.
8. Pour this onto the greased platter and keep it in the steamer to steam for eight to ten minutes.
9. Check with a knife. If the knife comes out clean, it is cooked.
10. Sprinkle some finely chopped coriander leaves and serve hot with green chutney.

Chef's Tip : You can also put crushed peppercorn or red chilli powder over the dhokla. It is best enjoyed with ghee if desired.

13

DHOKLA

FISH RAWA FINGERS

INGREDIENTS

Fish (ghole/bekti) fillet ...300 gms

Ginger paste ....1 tblspn

Garlic paste ....1 tblspn

Salt .... as per taste

Lemon juice ....2 tblspns

Red chilli powder ....2 tspns

Rice flour (coarse) ....½ cup

Oil .... to deep fry

METHOD OF PREPARATION

1 Clean the fish and cut into fingers (3" x ½" x ½").

2 Marinate the fish fingers in a mixture of ginger-garlic paste, salt and lemon juice for half an hour.

3 Mix red chilli powder, salt and coarse rice flour.

4 Remove the fish fingers from the first marinate and roll them in seasoned red chilli and rice flour mixture.

5 Heat oil in a kadai and deep fry in hot oil till crisp and done.

6 Remove onto an absorbent paper to remove excess oil.

7 Serve hot with garlic chutney.

HARA BHARA KABAB

INGREDIENTS

Boiled potatoes...3-4 medium sized
Boiled green peas ....¾ cup
Spinach ....100 gms
Chopped green chillies ....1 tblspn
Chopped green coriander..2 tblspns

Chopped ginger ....1 tblspn
Chaat masala ....1 tspn
Salt ....as per taste
Cornflour (cornstarch) ...2 tblspns
Oil ....for deep frying

METHOD OF PREPARATION

1. Peel and grate boiled potatoes.
2. Mash boiled green peas.
3. Blanch spinach leaves in plenty of salted boiling water, refresh in cold water and squeeze out excess water. Finely chop.
4. Mix grated potatoes, peas and spinach. Add chopped green chillies, chopped green coriander, chopped ginger, chaat masala and salt. Add cornflour for binding.
5. Divide the mixture into twenty five equal portions. Shape each portion into a ball and then press it in between your palms to give it a flat tikki shape.
6. Heat oil in a kadai. Deep-fry the tikkis in hot oil for three to four minutes.

Chef's Tip : You may also shallow fry hara bhara kabab on a griddle plate or a tawa. It is recommended that you do not use colour in this recipe. If you feel you may increase the quantity of spinach leaves to give a dark green colour. In that case add a little more cornflour/cornstarch for binding.

INGREDIENTS

Flour (*maida*) ....1 cup

Semolina (*rawa*) ....2 tblspns

Salt ....as per taste

Ghee ....¼ cup

Green chillies 3

Oil ....2 tblspns + to fry

Cumin seeds ....1 tspn

Minced mutton (*kheema*) ..... 400 gms

Chopped ginger ....2 tblspns

Red chilli powder .... 1 tspn

Coriander powder ....1 tblspn

Cumin powder .... 1 tspn

Yogurt ....¾ cup

Garam masala powder ....1 tspn

Chopped coriander leaves ....2 tblspns

METHOD OF PREPARATION

1 Knead together maida, rawa (suji), salt and ghee with warm water to make a stiff dough. Keep covered for thirty minutes. Divide the dough into twenty balls.

2 Chop green chillies fine. Keep aside.

3 Heat two tblspns of oil in a kadai and add cumin seeds. When they start crackling slightly, add kheema and sauté till half cooked. Add a little water if required.

4 Add chopped ginger, green chillies, red chilli powder, coriander and cumin powders and salt and mix well. Cover and cook on low heat for fifteen minutes. Then add yogurt. Cook on high flame for ten minutes, stirring continuously. Cook till the kheema is fully cooked and completely dry.

5 Sprinkle garam masala and coriander leaves and mix well. Cool. Divide into twenty portions.

6 Roll the dough balls into small puris (three inch diameter). Place a kheema portion in the centre. Apply a little water on the areas a little away from the edges and shape like a potli or modak. Seal by pressing them.

7 Deep fry in medium hot oil till golden brown.

8 Serve with chutney of your preference.

KHEEMA POTLI

KHAMAN DHOKLA

INGREDIENTS

Gramflour (besan) .... 2 cups
Yogurt ....1 cup
Chopped green chillies ....1 tblspn
Chopped ginger .... 1 tblspn
Turmeric powder .... ½ tspn
Salt .... as per taste

Soda bi-carbonate (baking soda) ....1 tspn
Oil ....2 tblspns
Lemon 1
Mustard seeds .... 1 tspn
Chopped green coriander ....2 tblspn
Grated fresh coconut ....¼ cup

METHOD OF PREPARATION

1 Take gramflour in a bowl. Add beaten yogurt and warm water. Whisk nicely so that no lumps remain. The mixture should be of a slightly thick consistency. Add salt and leave it covered to ferment for three to four hours.

2 Grind green chillies and ginger into a paste.

3 When the gramflour and yogurt mixture has fermented, add ground chillies and ginger. Add turmeric powder and correct seasoning.

4 Keep the steamer ready on the flame.

5 Grease the dhokla mould/shallow cake tin or a thali with a little oil. In a small bowl take one teaspoon of soda bi-carbonate, one teaspoon oil and juice of a lemon. Mix and add to the gramflour mixture.

6 Pour the batter into the greased mould and steam for ten to twelve minutes. Proceed similarly with rest of the batter.

7 When a little cool, cut into squares and keep in a serving bowl/plate.

8 Heat oil in a small pan. Add mustard seeds. When the seeds begin to crackle remove and pour over the dhoklas.

9 Serve, garnished with chopped green coriander leaves and grated coconut.

INGREDIENTS

Gram flour *(besan)* .... 1 ¼ cups
Ginger ....1 one inch piece
Green chillies 2
Yogurt ....1 cup
Salt ....as per taste
Turmeric powder ....½ tspn
Lemon juice ....1 tblspn

Water .... ½ cups
Oil ....4 tblspns
Mustard seeds .... 1 tspn
Asafoetida ....a pinch
Grated coconut ....2 tblspns
Chopped coriander leaves .. 2 tblspns

METHOD OF PREPARATION

1 Sieve the besan and keep in a bowl. Grind ginger and green chillies. Grease the reverse side of a few thalis or marble tabletop.

2 Make buttermilk with yogurt and water.

3 Mix the besan with ginger, green chillies, salt, turmeric powder, lemon juice and buttermilk. Take care that there are no lumps.

4 Cook this mixture over fire till it thickens into a thick batter. Stir constantly.

5 Quickly spread the mixture over the greased inverted thalis or marbled top as thinly as possible while the batter is still hot.

6 When cool, roll the layer towards you and cut into 1″ pieces.

7 Heat oil and add mustard seeds. When they splutter, add asafoetida and pour over the pieces.

8 Serve garnished with grated coconut and chopped coriander leaves.

Chef's Tip : Making Khandvi is an art, it takes some practise to get the correct consistency after cooking. Try small portions first.

KHANDVI

18

MEDU VADA

INGREDIENTS

Black gram, skinless *(urad dal)* .... 1 cup

Salt .... as per taste

Asafoetida ....¼ tspn

Curry leaves 8-10

Cumin powder .... 1 tspn

Crushed black peppercorns ....1 tspn

Oil ....to deep fry

METHOD OF PREPARATION

1 Wash and soak urad dal for six hours. Grind into a fine paste.

2 Add salt, asafoetida, curry leaves, cumin powder and crushed peppercorns to the batter and mix well.

3 Heat oil in a kadai.

4 Wet your palms and take batter into the palms. Shape into balls and make a hole with the thumb in the centre like a doughnut.

5 Deep-fry this in medium hot oil until golden brown and crisp.

6 Serve hot with sambhar and coconut chutney.

MIRCHI VADA

INGREDIENTS

Large green chillies 16

Boiled potatoes ....500 gms

Red chilli powder ....1 tblspn

Garam masala powder ....1 tblspn

Chaat masala ....1 tspn

Chopped green coriander ....1 tblspn

Salt ....as per taste

For batter

Gram flour (besan) .... 1 cup

Baking powder ....1 tspn

Red chilli powder ....1 tspn

Salt ....as per taste

Oil ....for deep-frying

METHOD OF PREPARATION

1   Slit green chillies and remove seeds.

2   Peel and grate boiled potatoes and add red chilli powder, garam masala powder, chaat masala, green coriander and salt. Mash and mix well. Divide this into sixteen equal portions.

3   Stuff a little of this mixture into the green chillies and also cover the chillies with this potato mixture.

4   Now prepare a thick batter using besan, baking powder, red chilli powder, salt and about one cup of water. Let the batter stand for ten minutes.

5   Heat oil in a kadai to a moderate temperature. Dip stuffed green chillies into the besan batter and deep fry until golden brown.

Chef's Tip : Select large sized green chillies for this recipe. It will not only give it a nice definite shape but also will not be very hot.

INGREDIENTS

Split green gram, skinless (*moong dal*)...1 cup
Cumin seeds ....1 tspn
Green chillies 2
Asafoetida ....a pinch
Salt ....as per taste
Cottage cheese (*paneer*) ....100 gms

Chopped onion...........................½ cup
Chopped tomato ....½ cup
Chopped coriander leaves ..... 2 tblspns
Red chilli powder ....½ tspn
Oil ....to shallow fry

METHOD OF PREPARATION

1 Pick, clean and wash moong dal. Soak moong dal in two cups of water for two hours. Grind soaked moong dal with cumin seeds and green chillies. Dissolve asafoetida in two tablespoons of water and mix it into the dal batter. Add salt and mix well.

2 Grate paneer and mix chopped onion, chopped tomato and chopped coriander leaves with this. Season with salt and red chilli powder. Keep aside.

3 Heat oil in a tawa or a frying pan. Spoon about one ¾ katori of batter onto the tawa and spread it to make a pancake with a diameter of about four to five inches. Shallow fry for about half a minute.

4 Sprinkle about two tablespoons of the paneer topping over the chillah. Spoon a little oil on the sides of the chillah and cook for fifteen seconds on medium heat.

5 Turn the chillah over and let it cook on the other side for two minutes on low to medium heat. Spoon oil on the sides of the chillah and turn it over. Cook for another minute on moderately high heat. Serve hot with mint chutney or chutney of your choice.

21

MOONG KE CHEELAY

INGREDIENTS

Boneless chicken ....600 gms

Split bengal gram (*chana dal*) ...... ½ cup

Ginger ....2 one inch pieces

Garlic .... 10-12 cloves

Onions ....2 medium sized

Coriander leaves ....2 tblspns

Mint leaves ....2 tblspns

Lemon juice ....2 tspns

Oil ....3 tblspns + to shallow fry

Cumin seeds ....½ tspn

Coriander seeds ....1 tspn

Peppercorns 5-6

Large cardamom 3-4

Red chilli powder ....1 tspn

Garam masala powder ....1 tspn

Mace and cardamom powder.... ½ tspn

Salt ....as per taste

METHOD OF PREPARATION

1 Wash the boneless chicken and drain out excess moisture. Soak chana dal for at least three hours.

2 Peel and chop the ginger and garlic finely.

3 Chop the onions, coriander leaves, mint leaves and mix them with lemon juice to make a stuffing. Divide into sixteen equal portions and keep aside.

4 Heat oil in a pan and add cumin seeds, coriander seeds, peppercorns and large cardamom, stir fry for half a minute on medium heat. Add chopped ginger, garlic and chilli powder.

5 Add boneless chicken and chana dal. Add two cups of water and bring to a boil. Reduce heat, cook covered till chana dal is completely cooked. Cook on high heat to dry out the mixture completely, stirring continuously.

6 Remove from heat and cool. Mince chicken and chana dal mixture to a smooth consistency.

7 Add garam masala powder, mace and cardamom powder and salt.

8 Mix well and check the seasoning.

9 Divide into sixteen equal portions. Flatten one in the palm of your hand and place a portion of onion stuffing in the centre. Shape into roundels and flatten slightly. Similarly shape the rest of the chicken mixture and stuffing.

10 Shallow fry till golden brown.

11 Serve hot with onion lachcha and mint chutney.

Chef's Tip: After cooking chicken mixture, if it is too moist, add roasted gram flour (besan) or powdered roasted chana dal as per your requirement.

MURGH KE SHAMI

PANEER KOLIWADA

INGREDIENTS

Cottage cheese *(paneer)*....300 gms
Gram flour *(besan)* ....½ cup
Cumin powder .... ½ tspn
Yogurt ....2 tblspns
Kashmiri red chilli powder.....2 tspn
Salt ....as per taste

Ginger paste .... 1 tblspn
Garlic paste ....1 tblspn
Lemon juice ....2 tblspns
Oil ....to fry
Chaat masala....................½ tspn

METHOD OF PREPARATION

1   Cut the paneer into finger size pieces (3" x ½" x ½").
2   Prepare a thick batter with besan, cumin powder, yogurt, red chilli powder, salt, ginger paste, garlic paste and lemon juice.
3   Marinate the paneer pieces in this batter for half an hour.
4   Heat oil in a kadai and deep fry the paneer pieces till crisp on the outside.
5   Serve hot, sprinkled with chaat masala.

Chef's Tip : To make Paneer koliwada extra crisp, add a tablespoon of cornstarch/ cornflour to the batter.

INGREDIENTS

Colocasia *(arbi)* leaves.................. 12

Gram flour *(besan)* ....1 ½ cups

Turmeric .... 1 tspn

Coriander powder ....2 tspns

Red chilli powder ....1 tspn

Cumin powder ....1 tspn

Sesame powder .... 2 tspns

Grated coconut .... ¼ cup

Salt ....as per taste

Green chillies paste ....1 tspn

Ginger paste ....1 tspn

Oil ....4 tblspns

Jaggery ....100 gms

Tamarind pulp .... 2 tblspns

Mustard seeds ....1 tspn

Chopped coriander leaves ..4 tblspns

Asafoetida ....¼ tspn

METHOD OF PREPARATION

1 Remove the thick stem from the leaves. Wash leaves and keep aside.

2 In a bowl take gram flour, turmeric powder coriander powder, cumin powder, red chilli powder, sesame powder, salt, green chillies' paste, ginger paste and two tblspns oil and mix well.

3 Mix the tamarind pulp and jaggery and add to the above mixture to make a paste.

4 Now spread the paste evenly on the back of each leaf, fold over the two sides and then roll.

5 Form into six inch rolls, making sure that all the batter is inside the leaf. Place the rolls on a sieve and steam.

6 Steam for about thirty to forty minutes or till cooked. Remove and let it cool. Cut into half centimetre thick pieces.

7 Heat oil in a kadai. Add mustard seeds.When they begin to crackle add asafoetida and then put in the steamed rolls. Sauté till golden brown.

8 Serve hot, garnished with grated coconut and coriander leaves.

Murgh ke shami

Malai kofta curry

Beans foogath

Dum ki arbi

RICE PAKORAS

INGREDIENTS

Gram flour (besan) ....½ cup
Cooked rice ....2 cups
Chopped green chillies ......1 tblspn
Chopped onion ....½ cup
Chopped green coriander ...1 tblspn

Chopped ginger ....1 tblspn
Chaat masala ....1 tspn
Salt ....as per taste
Oil .... for deep-frying

METHOD OF PREPARATION

1 Mix all the above ingredients except oil. Add one-fourth cup water to make a thick batter.

2 Heat oil in a kadai to a moderate heat.

3 Spoon the batter into hot oil by using a tablespoon and deep fry till light golden brown.

4 Drain on a paper napkin to remove excess oil and fry once again in very hot oil briefly.

5 Serve hot with chutney of your choice.

Chef's Tip : For this recipe you may also use leftover cooked rice.

SABUDANA VADA

INGREDIENTS

Sago *(sabudana)* ....1 ½ cups

Potatoes ....3 medium sized

Roasted peanuts ....1 cup

Green chillies 3

Chopped coriander leaves ...2 tblspns

Lemon juice ....1 tblspn

Salt ....as per taste

Oil ....to fry

METHOD OF PREPARATION

1 Soak the sabudana (in enough water to cover it) for about two hours. Drain out excess water. Boil, peel and mash the potatoes.

2 Coarsely grind the roasted peanuts. Finely chop the green chillies.

3 Mix together sabudana, mashed potatoes, ground peanuts, chopped green chillies and green coriander, lemon juice and salt. Mix thoroughly.

4 Form into sixteen lemon sized balls, flatten between your palms and deep fry in hot oil till golden brown.

5 Serve hot with chutney of your choice.

INGREDIENTS

For dough
Flour (*maida*) .... 1 cup
Carom seeds (*ajwain*) (optional)....½ tspn
Ghee/oil ....3 tblspns
Salt .... as per taste

For stuffing
Shelled green peas ....½ cup
Oil ....2 tblspns + for frying
Cumin seeds .... 1 tspn

Chopped ginger ....1 tspn
Chopped green chillies ....1 tspn
Potato cubes (½ cm) ....2 cups
Red chilli powder.......................1 tspn
Salt .... as per taste
Dry mango powder (*amchur*) .....1 tspn
Garam masala powder ....1 tspn
Chopped coriander leaves ....1 tblspn

METHOD OF PREPARATION

1 Mix the dough ingredients. Add water little by little and make a hard dough. Keep it under a wet cloth for ten to fifteen minutes.

2 Cook green peas in salted boiling water till soft. Refresh in cold water. Drain out excess water.

3 Heat oil in a pan, add cumin seeds and when they start to change colour, add chopped ginger, chopped green chillies and diced potatoes. Add red chilli powder, salt, amchur and garam masala powder. Stir well.

4 Sprinkle water and cook covered till potatoes are done. Add shelled green peas and mix well.

5 Divide the dough into sixteen equal portions and roll them into balls. Apply a little flour and roll them into four inch diameter elongated diskettes.

6 Cut into half, apply water on the edges. Shape into a cone and stuff it with the potato and peas filling. Seal the edges and deep fry in medium hot oil till crisp and golden brown.

7 Serve hot with tamarind chutney.

27

VEGETABLE
SAMOSA

INGREDIENTS

Chicken	1 kg	Oil	½ cup
Poppy seeds (khus khus)	2 tspns	Onion	1 large
Grated coconut	½	Ginger chopped	2 tspns
Fennel seeds	1 tspn	Garlic chopped	2 tspns
Coriander seeds	1 tspn	Star anise	½
Cumin seeds	½ tspn	Red chilli powder	1 tspn
Whole red chillies	6-8	Tomatoes	3 medium sized
Cinnamon	1 one inch stick	Lemon	1
Green cardamom	3	Curry leaves	10-12
Cloves	2	Fresh coriander	for garnish
Turmeric powder	½ tspn	Salt	as per taste

METHOD OF PREPARATION

1 Clean the chicken, remove skin and cut into twelve pieces.

2 Chop the onions and tomatoes separately.

3 Roast the whole red chillies, grated coconut, poppy seeds, coriander seeds, cumin seeds, green cardamom, cloves, cinnamon, star anise, fennel seeds in oil and grind to a paste along with ginger and garlic.

4 Heat oil in a degchi and fry the onions till golden. Add the curry leaves and the ground paste and sauté for some time. Add the tomatoes, red chilli powder and turmeric powder.

5 Add chicken and mix. Cook for five minutes and then add two cups of water, lemon juice, cover and cook till the chicken is done.

6 Serve hot, garnished with coriander leaves and accompanied with boiled rice or parantha.

Chef's Tip : In some regions this dish is cooked without coconut. You may try that variation as per your preference.

CHICKEN
CHETTINAD

CHICKEN CURRY

INGREDIENTS

Chicken .... 800 gms	Ginger paste .... 1 tblspn
Onions .... 4-5 medium sized	Garlic paste .... 1 tblspn
Tomatoes .... 4-5 medium sized	Turmeric powder .... ½ tspn
Chopped coriander leaves ....1 tblspn	Coriander powder .... 2 tblspns
Ghee/Oil ....4 tblspns	Cumin powder .... 2 tspns
Cinnamon .... 1 one inch stick	Red chilli powder .... 1 tspn
Cloves 4-5	Salt .... as per taste
Green cardamom 4-5	Garam masala powder .... 1 tspn

METHOD OF PREPARATION

1. Clean the chicken, remove skin and cut into eight pieces.
2. Peel onions and grate or finely chop. Wash and puree the tomatoes.
3. Heat ghee/oil in a thick-bottomed pan. Add cinnamon, cloves and green cardamom. Stir-fry for half a minute. Sauté grated onion till it is golden brown. Add ginger and garlic pastes and continue to cook for two to three minutes, stirring constantly.
4. Add turmeric powder, coriander powder, cumin powder and red chilli powder. Mix well.
5. Add pureed tomato, stir. Cook till oil separates from the masala. Add the chicken pieces and salt to taste. Cook on a high flame for five minutes. Add two cups of water, bring to a boil, cover and cook till the chicken is fully done.
6. Sprinkle garam masala powder and garnish with chopped coriander leaves and serve hot.

Chef's Tip : You may add two tablespoons of cashewnut paste to the gravy to make it a little rich.

CHICKEN KANDHARI KOFTA

INGREDIENTS

Chicken mince .... 500 gms
Cinnamon powder .... ½ tspn
Salt .... as per taste
Oil .... 3 tblspns
Boiled onion paste .... ¾ cup
Ginger-garlic paste .... 1 tblspn
Coriander powder .... 1 tblspn

Red chilli powder .... 1 tspn
Tomato puree .... ½ cup
Cashewnut paste .... ²/₃ cup
Garam masala powder ... ½ tspn
Pomegranate syrup ..... 2 tblspns
Fresh cream .... ½ cup

METHOD OF PREPARATION

1. Mix cinnamon powder, one teaspoon salt and chicken mince thoroughly. Divide into twelve equal portions. Shape them into balls (koftas). Keep the koftas aside.

2. Heat oil in a pan. Add boiled onion paste and cook till onions turn pink. Add ginger-garlic paste. Sauté for a minute, then add coriander powder and red chilli powder.

3. Stir in tomato puree and cashewnut paste dissolved in a little water. Cook for five minutes on a high flame, stirring constantly.

4. Add one and half cups of water, bring it to a boil. Add chicken koftas and cook for ten minutes, stirring occasionally. Add garam masala powder and pomegranate syrup. Correct seasoning. Simmer for five minutes. Stir in fresh cream.

5. Serve with naan or parantha.

Chef's Tip : Make cashewnut paste by soaking half-cup cashewnuts in water for half an hour. Grind it to a smooth paste. You do not need to use expensive full cashewnuts, you can use cashewnut pieces (tukda).

INGREDIENTS

Chicken 1 (800gms)
Lemon juice ....1 tblspn
Kashmiri red chilli powder...........1 tspn
Salt ....as per taste

For Marination
Yogurt ....1 cup
Salt ....as per taste
Garlic paste ....2 tblspns
Garam masala powder ....½ tspn
Buttter (for basting) ....2 tblspns
Kashmiri chilli powder ....1 tspn
Ginger paste ....2 tblspns
Lemon juice ....2 tblspns
Mustard oil ....2 tblspns

For Makhani gravy
Butter ....50 gms
Ginger paste ....1 tblspn
Chopped green chillies ....1 tspn
Red chilli powder ....1 tblspn
Salt ....as per taste
Dried fenugreek leaves (*kasoori methi*) ...½ tspn
Whole garam masala ....1 tblspn
Garlic paste ....1 tblspn
Tomato puree ....400 gms
Garam masala powder ....½ tspn
Sugar/Honey ....2 tblspns
Fresh cream ....1 cup

METHOD OF PREPARATION

1. Skin and clean the chicken. Make incisions with a sharp knife on breast and leg pieces.

2. Apply a mixture of red chilli powder, lemon juice and salt to the chicken and leave aside for half an hour.

3. Hang the yogurt in a muslin cloth for fifteen to twenty minutes to remove extra water. Then add red chilli powder, salt, ginger-garlic paste, lemon juice, garam masala powder and mustard oil.

4. Apply this marinade to the chicken pieces and refrigerate for three to four hours.

5. Put the chicken on to a skewer and cook in a moderately hot tandoor or a preheated oven (200 degrees Celsius) for ten to twelve minutes or until almost done. Baste it with butter and cook for another two minutes. Remove and keep aside.

6. Heat butter in a pan. Add whole garam masala. Let it crackle.Then add ginger-garlic paste and chopped green chillies.Cook for two minutes.

7. Add tomato puree, red chilli powder, garam masala powder, salt and one cup of water. Bring to a boil. Reduce heat and simmer for ten minutes. Add sugar or honey and powdered kasoori methi.

8. Add cooked tandoori chicken pieces. Simmer for five minutes and then add fresh cream.

9. Serve hot with naan or parantha.

Chef's Tip : Heat kasoori methi in the oven for sometime or broil kasoori methi on a tawa/ griddle plate to make it crisp. It can easily be crushed to a powder with your hand.

CHICKEN MAKHANI

CHICKEN XACUTI

INGREDIENTS

Chicken .... 800 gms
Onions ....2 medium sized
Grated coconut .... 1 cup
Cinnamon ....2 one inch sticks
Cloves 6
Dry red chillies 4
Turmeric powder ....½ tsp
Poppy seeds (*khus khus*) ....2 tblspns
Carom seeds (*ajwain*) .... 1 tspn
Cumin seeds .... 1 tspn

Peppercorns ....1 tspn
Fennel seeds (*saunf*) .... 1 tspn
Star anise (*Phoolchakri/badiyan*) 4
Coriander seeds .... 1 ½ tblspns
Garlic ....4-6 cloves
Groundnut oil .... $^1/_3$ cup
Salt ....as per taste
Tamarind pulp ....1 tblspn
Grated nutmeg ....¼ tspn

METHOD OF PREPARATION

1. Wash, clean, remove the skin and cut chicken into twelve pieces. The size of the pieces used is normally a little smaller than the one used for chicken curry.
2. Peel and chop the onions.
3. Heat a little oil and slightly brown the grated coconut and keep aside.
4. Now dry roast cinnamon, cloves, red chillies, turmeric, khus khus, ajwain, cumin seeds, peppercorns, fennel seeds, star anise and coriander seeds till a nice aroma is given out. Grind to a paste together with garlic and coconut.
5. Heat the remaining oil in a thick-bottomed pan and sauté the finely chopped onions till brown.
6. Add the masala paste and cook till oil separates. Add the chicken pieces and sauté for sometime. Add two cups of water and salt, bring to a boil and add tamarind pulp and grated nutmeg.
7. Simmer for five minutes and serve hot with Goan pav or Goan rice.

INGREDIENTS

Chicken .... 1 (800 gms)	Bay leaves 2
Ginger ....1 two inch piece	Coriander powder ....1 tblspn
Garlic ....6-8 cloves	Cumin powder ....1 tspn
Green chillies 3-4	Mace powder ....¼ tspn
Almonds 15-20	Green cardamom powder ....¼ tspn
Onions ....2 medium sized	Large cardamom powder ....½ tspn
Ghee ....4 tspns + to fry onion	Cinnamon powder ....¼ tspn
Yogurt ....1 ½ cups	Fresh cream ....½ cup
Salt ....as per taste	

METHOD OF PREPARATION

1 Wash, clean chicken and cut into eight pieces. Peel and wash ginger and garlic. Make a paste of ginger, garlic and green chillies.

2 Soak the almonds in warm water for fifteen to twenty minutes. Peel and grind into a fine paste.

3 Slice the onions. Deep fry in ghee till golden brown and grind to a fine paste.

4 Marinate the chicken pieces in yogurt, ginger-garlic-green chilli paste and salt for two hours.

5 Heat ghee in a degchi. Add bay leaves. Add the marinated chicken and cook till the gravy starts boiling. Add coriander and cumin powders and onion paste and almond paste dissolved in half a cup of water. Stir.

6 Cover the degchi with a tight-fitting lid or cover with aluminium foil so that the steam does not escape. Simmer for fifteen minutes. Alternatively you can cover the degchi and seal using wheat flour (*atta*) dough. Cook over low heat till the flavours are given out.

7 Uncover the degchi and sprinkle the mace, green cardamom, large cardamom and cinnamon powders. Stir in fresh cream.

8 Serve hot.

Chef's Tip : If the degchi is sealed with the atta dough, it is said, as soon as the dish is ready, the degchi will give out an aroma and call the person cooking the dish to give the finishing touches.

33

DUM MURGH

KOZHI VARTHA KARI

INGREDIENTS

Chicken ....1 kg	Turmeric powder .... 1 tspn
Onions ....2 medium sized	Salt .... as per taste
Tomatoes ....3 medium sized	Oil ....5 tblspns
Peppercorns .... 3 tspns	Curry leaves 12-15
Dried red chillies 2	Coriander powder .... 2 tspns
Ginger .... 1 two inch piece	Tamarind pulp .... 1 tblspn
Garlic ....6-8 cloves	Garam masala powder .... 1 tspn
Red chilli powder ....1 tspn	Chopped coriander leaves .... 2 tblspns
Lemon juice ....1 tblspn	

METHOD OF PREPARATION

1 Wash, clean and cut chicken into sixteen pieces. This chicken dish tastes better with chicken cut into smaller pieces. You may also use small boneless chicken pieces.

2 Peel and chop the onions. Wash and finely chop the tomatoes. Crush the peppercorns coarsely.

3 Make a paste of dried red chillies, ginger and garlic. Marinate the chicken pieces in ginger-garlic paste, red chilli powder, lemon juice, turmeric powder and salt for three hours.

4 Heat a little oil in a thick-bottomed pan and sauté the marinated chicken on high heat till chicken pieces are dry and a little brown. Take out chicken pieces and keep aside.

5 Add the remaining oil in the pan and fry the chopped onions till brown. Add curry leaves and stir well. Add tomatoes, salt and coriander powder and cook till oil leaves the masala.

6 Add the chicken and a little water. Cover and cook till the chicken is done and the masala coats the pieces.

7 Add tamarind pulp dissolved in half cup of water. Simmer for ten minutes, stirring occasionally. Add garam masala powder. Mix lightly.

8 Adjust the seasoning and add coarsely ground peppercorns. Garnish with chopped coriander leaves and serve hot.

34

INGREDIENTS

Chicken ....1 (800 gms)	Saffron .... a generous pinch
Ginger ....1 one inch piece	Mawa (*khoya*)..................... ½ cup
Garlic ....6-8 cloves	Ghee/Oil ....3 tblspns
Green chillies 3-4	Bay leaves 2
Onions .... 2 medium sized	Cashewnut paste ....¾ cup
Salt .... as per taste	Fresh cream ....¾ cup
Turmeric powder ....½ tspn	Mace powder ....¼ tspn
Yogurt ....½ cup	Green cardamom powder ...¼ tspn
Milk ....½ cup	Garam masala powder ......½ tspn

METHOD OF PREPARATION

1 Clean the chicken, remove skin and cut into eight pieces. Wash and peel ginger. Make a paste of ginger, garlic and green chillies. Peel and roughly slice the onions. Boil in a cup of water, drain out excess water and grind into a fine paste.

2 Marinate chicken in ginger, garlic and green chilli paste with salt, turmeric and yogurt for one hour.

3 Warm a little milk and dissolve the saffron in it. Crumble the mawa and mix it with the remaining milk.

4 Heat ghee or oil in a pan and add the bay leaves. Add the boiled onion paste, cook for five minutes. Add the chicken pieces and salt and stir fry on high heat for three minutes.

5 Add cashewnut paste dissolved in two cups of water and cook on high heat for ten minutes, stirring continuously. Add mawa and milk mixture and stir.

6 Cover and cook till chicken is almost cooked. This should take about five minutes on slow heat. Add half the cream, saffron-milk and cook over low flame for a while.

7 Sprinkle mace powder, cardamom powder and garam masala powder. Garnish with the remaining cream and serve hot.

SUNHERI MURGH

INGREDIENTS

Chicken ....1 (800 gms)
Kashmiri red chilli powder .... 1 tspn
Lemon juice ....1 tblspn
Salt .... as per taste

For Marination

Yogurt ....200 gms
Kashmiri red chilli powder .... 1 tspn
Salt .... as per taste
Ginger paste ....2 tblspns

Garlic paste ....2 tblspns
Lemon juice ....2 tblspns
Garam masala powder ....½ tspn
Mustard oil ....2 tblspns
Butter ....for basting
Chaat masala ....½ tspn

For garnishing

Onion rings and Lemon wedges

METHOD OF PREPARATION

1. Skin, wash and clean the chicken. Make incisions with a sharp knife on breast and leg pieces.

2. Apply a mixture of kashmiri red chilli powder, lemon juice and salt to the chicken and keep it aside for half an hour.

3. Remove whey of yogurt by hanging it in a muslin cloth for fifteen to twenty minutes. Mix Kashmiri red chilli powder, salt, ginger-garlic paste, lemon juice, garam masala powder and mustard oil to the yogurt.

4. Apply this marinade onto the chicken pieces and refrigerate for three to four hours.

5. Put the chicken onto the skewers and cook in a moderately hot tandoor or a pre-heated oven (200 degrees Celsius) for ten to twelve minutes or until almost done. Baste it with butter and cook for another four minutes.

6. Sprinkle chaat masala powder and serve with four onion rings and lemon wedges.

Chef's Tip : To make Chicken tikka, use boneless chicken pieces cut into 1½" cubes and proceed same as Tandoori chicken.

TANDOORI CHICKEN

ACHARI GOSHT

INGREDIENTS

Mutton/Lamb	800 gms	Cloves	5
Onions	4 medium sized	Mustard oil	100 ml
Tomatoes	4 medium sized	Chopped ginger	2 tblspns
Whole red chillies	8	Chopped garlic	2 tblspns
Mustard seeds	1 tspn	Turmeric powder	1 tspn
Fenugreek seeds	½ tspn	Red chilli powder	1 tspn
Cumin seeds	½ tspn	Salt	as per taste
Fennel seeds (*saunf*)	1 tspn	Chopped coriander leaves	½ cup
Onion seeds (*kalonji*)	1 tspn	Lemon	1

METHOD OF PREPARATION

1   Wash and cut the mutton into 1 ½″ sized pieces. Peel and chop the onions. Chop the tomatoes.

2   Roast the whole spices (mustard seeds, cumin seeds, onion seeds, whole red chillies, fenugreek seeds, fennel seeds and cloves) separately and grind together coarsely.

3   Heat mustard oil in a thick-bottomed pan to smoking point. Cool and again heat the oil and cook the onions till brown. Add the chopped ginger and garlic. Mix well. Add coarsely ground masala powder. Cook for half a minute, stirring constantly.

4   Add mutton, cook on high heat till mutton pieces are fairly brown.

5   Add turmeric powder, red chilli powder and salt and mix well. Cook till oil leaves the masala. Add sufficient quantity of water (about 2 ½ cups), bring it to a boil and cover. Cook till the mutton is almost done.

6   Add chopped tomatoes and cook on medium flame for ten minutes or till mutton is fully cooked. Stir occasionally. Stir in juice of a lemon.

7   Adjust the seasoning and serve hot, garnished with coriander leaves.

Chef's Tip : Pressure cook mutton/lamb to cook it in less time.

KHEEMA HARA DHANIA

INGREDIENTS

Mutton mince *(kheema)* ...... 600 gms
Ginger................... 1 two inch piece
Garlic .... 10-12 cloves
Green chillies 4-5
Chopped coriander leaves ..... 1 cup
Onions .... 3 medium sized
Lemons 2
Peppercorn .... 1 tspn
Eggs 4

Ghee or oil .... 3 tblspns
Cumin seeds .... 1 tspn
Green cardamom 3-4
Cinnamon .... 1 one inch stick
Cloves 4-6
Coriander powder .... 1 tblspn
Salt .... as per taste
Garam masala powder ...... 1 tspn
Chopped mint leaves ...... 1 tblspn

METHOD OF PREPARATION

1 Wash and remove all the excess water from mutton mince.
2 Peel and chop ginger and garlic. Wash chillies and grind ginger, garlic, green chillies and half cup coriander leaves to a paste. Peel onions and chop them finely. Take out juice of two lemons and keep aside.
3 Crush peppercorn coarsely. Boil eggs in boiling hot water for twelve minutes. Cool, peel and cut into quarters. Keep aside.
4 Heat ghee/oil in a thick-bottomed pan and add cumin seeds, green cardamom, cinnamon stick and cloves. Stir for ten seconds and then add chopped onion. Cook till onions turn golden brown. Add ginger-garlic-green chilli-green coriander paste and sauté for half a minute.
5 Add mutton mince and cook on high heat, stirring continuously, for ten minutes. Add coriander powder and mix well. Now stir in one and half cups of water and bring it to boil, reduce heat, cover and simmer for half an hour, stirring occasionally. In case the mutton mince is still not cooked, add some more water and cook on low heat till mince is fully cooked.
6 Add salt, garam masala powder and lemon juice. Add remaining chopped coriander leaves and chopped mint leaves. Mix well and serve hot, decorated with boiled eggs.

INGREDIENTS

Mutton liver (*kaleji*) ....200 gms
Turmeric powder ....1 tspn
Onions ....2 medium sized
Tomatoes ....4 medium sized
Green chillies 3-4
Mutton mince (*kheema*)...400 gms
Butter or oil ....3 tblspns
Cumin seeds ....1 tspn

Ginger paste ....1 tblspn
Garlic paste ....1 tblspn
Coriander powder .... 2 tspns
Red chilli powder .... 1 tspn
Rock salt ....½ tspn
Salt ....as per taste
Coriander leaves ....2 tblspns

METHOD OF PREPARATION

1 Clean, wash and boil the liver in water to which half teaspoon turmeric powder has been added. Cook for five minutes. Drain excess water and dice into half inch pieces when a little cold.

2 Peel and chop the onions. Wash and chop tomatoes and green chillies.

3 Wash the kheema and drain away all the excess water.

4 Heat butter or oil in a thick-bottomed pan and add cumin seeds, cook till cumin seeds change their colour slightly. Add chopped onions and sauté till golden brown. Stir constantly. Add ginger and garlic pastes and chopped green chillies. Cook for half a minute on medium heat.

5 Add mince and cook on high heat till mince turns a good brown. Add coriander powder, remaining turmeric powder, red chilli powder and cook on medium heat to roast spices nicely. Add tomatoes and cook till oil leaves the masala.

6 Add liver pieces and one cup of water, bring it to a boil, reduce heat and simmer for fifteen to twenty minutes, till mince is fully cooked.

7 Add rock salt, salt and some of the chopped coriander leaves. Cook for a while.

8 Serve hot, garnished with the remaining coriander leaves.

Chef's Tip : This is a dry dish with hardly any gravy. The gravy for this dish is in the form of thick masala.

KHEEMA KALEJI

KOLHAPURI SUKKA MUTTON

INGREDIENTS

Mutton (leg or shoulder) ....1 kg
Garam masala powder ....1 tspn
Onions ....5 medium sized
Dry coconut (khopra) ....100 gms
Oil ... 3 tblspns and to deep fry sliced onions
Tomatoes ....4 medium sized
Turmeric powder .... ½ tspn

Salt ....as per taste
Garlic paste ....1 tblspn
Ginger paste ....1 tblspn
Green cardamom powder ....½ tspn
Red chilli powder
(preferably Sankeshwari) ....2 tspns

METHOD OF PREPARATION

1 Wash and clean mutton. Cut it into 1 ½″ sized pieces.

2 Grate khopra(dry coconut) and dry roast on a hot tawa(griddle) till light golden brown, stir constantly and ensure that it does not burn.

3 Peel onions and slice half of these and finely chop the rest. Wash, clean and finely chop tomatoes.

4 Heat oil in a kadai and deep fry sliced onions till it is golden brown. Remove on a paper towel and cool. Grind fried onions and roasted khopra with a little warm water, to a paste.

5 Rub salt and turmeric powder on mutton pieces. Pressure cook with two and half cups of water or boil with sufficient water till mutton is almost cooked.

6 Heat three table spoons oil in a thick-bottomed pan. Add chopped onions. Cook till golden brown. Stir in ginger and garlic pastes. Add chopped tomatoes and cook for five minutes. Add Sankeshwari red chilli powder and khopra and onion paste. Cook on high heat till oil leaves the sides of the pan or starts appearing on the edges of the masala.

7 Now add boiled mutton and salt. Stir constantly and cook further for ten minutes till the consistency of the gravy is thick and mutton pieces are nicely coated with the masala.

8 Flavour with green cardamom powder and garam masala powder.

Mixed vegetables in coconut milk

Mirchi ka salan

Tandoori chicken

Khandvi, Khaman Dhokla, Patra

MALBARI MUTTON

INGREDIENTS

Mutton ....800 gms	Green Cardamom 4-6
Onions ....2 medium sized	Cloves 6-8
Roughly chopped ginger ....2 tblspns	Bay leaves 2
Garlic cloves 12-15	Grated coconut ....¾ cup
Green chillies 3-4	Poppy seeds (*khus khus*) ....2 tblspns
Tomatoes ....3 medium sized	Black peppercorns 10-12
Oil ....½ cup	Mustard seeds ....½ tspn
Cumin seeds ....1 tspn	Curry leaves 10
Coriander seeds ....1 tblspn	Turmeric powder ....1 tspn
Dry red chillies 4-5	Red chilli powder ....½ tspn
Fenugreek seeds ....½ tspn	Salt ....as per taste
Cinnamon ....2 one inch sticks	

METHOD OF PREPARATION

1 Clean, wash and cut the mutton into 1 ½ " pieces.

2 Peel and slice the onions. Grind ginger, garlic and green chillies into a paste. Wash and chop the tomatoes.

3 Heat two table spoons of oil in a pan and add cumin seeds, coriander seeds, dry red chillies, fenugreek seeds, cinnamon, cardamom, cloves, and bay leaves. Stir fry for thirty seconds. Add the grated coconut, khus khus, pepper corns and cook till grated coconut changes its colour slightly. Remove from flame and then grind into a fine paste.

4 Heat remaining oil, add mustard seeds and curry leaves. Add sliced onions and sauté till golden brown. Add the mutton pieces and the ginger-garlic-green chilli paste. Cook on high heat for ten minutes, stirring continuously. Add turmeric powder, red chilli powder, salt and chopped tomatoes. Cook till oil leaves the masala.

5 Add four cups of water, bring it to a boil. Cover the pan and simmer for at least half an hour or till mutton is fully cooked.

6 Now add the masala paste and salt. Mix well. Add more water if required. Simmer for ten more minutes. Serve hot.

MANGO GOSHT

INGREDIENTS

Boneless lamb or mutton .....600 gms	Cinnamon ....1 one inch stick
Yogurt ....¾ cup	Grated onions ....1 cup
Dry mango powder (amchur) ..1 tspn	Ginger paste ....1 tblspn
Turmeric powder .... 1 tspn	Coriander powder ....1 tblspn
Oil .... 4 tblspns	Red chilli powder ....1 tblspn
Mustard seeds .... 1 tspn	Raw mango pieces (without skin)...½ cup
Curry leaves 8-10	Salt .... as per taste
Cloves 4-5	

42

METHOD OF PREPARATION

1. Clean, wash and cut lamb or mutton into one inch pieces. Marinate in a mixture of yogurt, amchur and turmeric powder.
2. Heat oil in a thick-bottomed pan. Add mustard seeds, curry leaves, cloves and cinnamon. Let mustard seeds crackle. Then add grated onions. Cook until onions are translucent.
3. Add marinated meat pieces and ginger paste. Cook on high flame, stirring constantly.
4. Add coriander powder, red chilli powder and raw mango pieces. Stir and cook for half a minute. Add two cups of water, bring it to boil. Cover the pan and let it simmer till meat pieces are tender.
5. Season with salt and again cook on a low flame till the gravy thickens.
6. Serve hot with bread of your choice.

INGREDIENTS

Lamb/mutton .... 800 gms

Oil/ghee .... 4 tblspns

Asafoetida .... 1¼ tspn

Cinnamon ....2 one inch pieces

Cloves 6-8

Black peppercorns 5-6

Large cardamom 4

Kashmiri Red chilli powder.....1 tblspn

Fennel (*saunf*) powder ....2 tspns

Ginger (*saunth*) powder ....1 tblspn

Coriander powder .... 1 tblspn

Yogurt .... 1 cup

METHOD OF PREPARATION

1 Clean, wash and cut lamb/mutton into medium sized pieces.

2 Heat oil in a thick-bottomed pan. Add asafoetida, cinnamon sticks, cloves, black peppercorns and large cardamoms. Sauté for half a minute.

3 Add lamb pieces and cook on a medium flame, stirring constantly till lamb pieces get a nice reddish brown colour. This may take twelve to fifteen minutes.

4 Sprinkle a little water and repeat cooking of meat for twelve to fifteen minutes on a low flame. Make sure to stir constantly and scrape all the sediments from the bottom of the pan.

5 Add red chilli powder, saunf powder, ginger powder, coriander powder and salt.

6 Add beaten yogurt and two cups of water. Cook covered till meat is tender. Stir occasionally.

Chef's Tip : Traditional Kashmiri Rogan Josh has a thin gravy and has a thick layer of fat/oil on top. This dish is enjoyed best with steaming hot boiled rice. Quality of meat plays an important role in this dish, so select meat with a lot of fat for Roganjosh.

ROGANJOSH

SAAG WALA GOSHT

INGREDIENTS

Lamb/Mutton	600 gms	Bay leaves	2
Spinach	500 gms	Whole garam masala	1 tblspn
Salt	as per taste	Cumin seeds	1 tspn
Green chillies	5	Sliced onions	1 cup
Garlic cloves	6-8	Ginger paste	1 tblspn
Ginger	1 one inch piece	Garlic paste	1 tblspn
Oil	4 tblspns	Red chilli powder	1 tspn

METHOD OF PREPARATION

1. Clean, wash and cut lamb/mutton into 1 ½" sized pieces.

2. Clean, remove stems and thoroughly wash spinach leaves. Boil spinach in salted boiling water for one minute. Drain well and coarsely grind it along with green chillies. Chop garlic cloves and keep aside. Peel ginger and cut into julienne (thin strips) and reserve for garnishing.

3. Heat oil in a thick-bottomed pan. Add bay leaves, whole garam masala and cumin seeds. When cumin seeds begin to change colour, add sliced onions. Cook till onions are translucent. Add chopped garlic, mix well.

4. Add ginger and garlic paste, red chilli powder and then add meat pieces. Cook on a high flame, stirring constantly. Add three cups of water and cook covered until meat is almost done.

5. Add salt and spinach and cook till meat is fully blended with spinach and is tender. Serve hot, garnished with ginger julienne.

Chef's Tip : Whole garam masala for this recipe consists of 6 green cardamom, 4 cloves, 2 black cardamom and one 1" stick of cinnamon.

INGREDIENTS

Boneless lamb/mutton ... 600 gms
Ghee/Oil .... 4 tblspns
Whole garam masala ..... 1 tblspn
Chopped onions .... 1 cup
Ginger-garlic paste .... 1 tblspn
Coriander powder .... 1 tblspn

Red chilli powder .... 1½ tspns
Salt .... as per taste
Yogurt .... ½ cup
Cashewnut paste .... ¼ cup
Garam masala powder ...... 1 tspn
Fresh cream .... ½ cup

METHOD OF PREPARATION

1. Cut boneless lamb/mutton into one inch cubes. Wash thoroughly and keep aside.
2. Heat ghee/oil in a thick bottomed pan and add whole garam masala. When it starts to crackle, add chopped onions and sauté till light pink.
3. Add ginger-garlic paste and cook for one minute. Stir constantly as the paste may stick to the bottom.
4. Add lamb/mutton pieces and cook on a high flame for three to four minutes stirring constantly.
5. Add coriander powder, red chilli powder and salt. Cook for another two to three minutes. Then add beaten yogurt and water.
6. When it starts to boil, reduce the flame, cover and cook till the lamb/mutton is cooked and tender.
7. Add cashewnut paste and garam masala powder. Cook for five more minutes on medium flame. Finish off with fresh cream. Simmer for ten minutes. Serve hot.

Chef's Tip : You may garnish Shahi korma with almonds, raisins and cashewnuts. Whole garam masala for this recipe comprises of 5 green cardamom, 4 cloves, 1 one inch cinnamon stick and half a blade of mace.

SHAHI KORMA

AMRITSARI FISH

INGREDIENTS

Boneless fish (preferably Surmai) ..... 600 gms	Carom seeds (*ajwain*) .... 1 tspn
Gram flour *(besan)* .... 1 cup	Red chilli powder .... 1 tblspn
Malt vinegar .... ½ cup	Oil .... for frying
Yogurt .... ½ cup	Ginger paste .... 2 tblspns
Salt .... as per taste	Chaat masala .... 1 tspn
Egg 1	Garlic paste .... 2 tblspns
Lemon juice .... 1 tblspn	Lemon wedges 6-8

METHOD OF PREPARATION

1 Clean, wash and cut fish into 1 ½ inch sized cubes. Marinate in vinegar for twenty minutes.

2 Remove from the vinegar and pat the fish dry.

3 Make a batter of besan, yogurt, egg, ajwain, salt, lemon juice, red chilli powder, ginger and garlic paste.

4 Keep the fish in this marinade for about twenty minutes.

5 Heat oil in a kadai and deep fry the fish till golden brown and crisp.

6 Serve hot, sprinkled with chaat masala and lemon wedges.

Chef's Tip : You could substitute malt vinegar with plain vinegar.

INGREDIENTS

River fish ....600 gms
Yogurt ....1 cup
Salt .... as per taste
Onions ....2 small sized
Green chillies 3

Ghee .... 2 tblspns
Bay leaves 2
Cloves 4-6
Green cardamom 3-4

METHOD OF PREPARATION

1 Clean, wash and cut fish into medium sized pieces. Whisk yogurt, add salt and marinate fish in this for twenty minutes.

2 Peel onions and grate them. Wash green chillies and slit them into two. Keep aside.

3 Take ghee in a kadai and add bay leaves, cloves and green cardamom. Cook for fifteen seconds. Add grated onions. Sauté for five to seven minutes.

4 Add halved green chillies and fish marinated in yogurt. Bring to a boil. Cover and cook on a low fire for seven to eight minutes.

Chef's Tip : Some people like this recipe cooked in mustard oil. If you wish to use mustard oil, bring it to a smoking point, cool it and then use as normal.

47

DOI MACHH

FISH AMBOTIK

INGREDIENTS

Onions ....2 medium sized
Pomfret fish .... 750 gms
Salt .... as per taste
Turmeric powder .... 1 tspn
Cumin seeds .... 1 tspn
Coriander seeds ....1 tblspn
Grated coconut .... 1 cup
Whole red chillies 8-10

Ginger ....1 one inch piece
Garlic ....8-10 cloves
Cloves 5
Cinnamon ....2 one inch sticks
Vinegar ....2 tblspns
Green chillies 4-5
Oil ....2 tblspns
Tamarind pulp ....3 tblspns

METHOD OF PREPARATION

1 Peel and chop the onions finely. Clean, wash and slice fish into half inch thick slices (darne). Marinate the fish slices with salt and turmeric powder for fifteen minutes. Slit green chillies into two.

2 Dry roast cumin and coriander seeds. Grind grated coconut, dried red chillies, cumin seeds, coriander seeds, peeled ginger, garlic, cloves and cinnamon with vinegar.

3 Heat oil in a pan, add chopped onions, sauté the onions till golden brown. Add ground coconut masala and cook on high flame for two minutes, stirring constantly.

4 Now add three cups of water and bring it to a boil. Stir in slit green chillies. Place marinated fish slices gently into the gravy and simmer for five minutes. Stir in tamarind pulp dissolved in half a cup of water. Add salt and cook on low fire for five minutes.

5 Serve hot with steamed rice.

Chef's Tip: If kokum is available, you may add 5-6 kokums soaked for half an hour in half a cup of water along with tamarind pulp. This recipe also works well with all kinds of shark fish, king fish and sting ray.

INGREDIENTS

River fish/Pomfret ....600 gms	Mustard seeds ....½ tspn
Salt ....as per taste	Curry leaves 8-10
Lemon juice ....2 tspns	Ginger paste ....2 tspns
Onions ....2 medium sized	Garlic paste ....2 tspns
Green chillies 3	Turmeric powder ....½ tspn
Oil ....1 tblspn	Coconut milk ....1 ½ cups

METHOD OF PREPARATION

1 Clean, wash and cut fish into medium sized pieces. Apply a little salt and lemon juice on fish pieces and keep aside for fifteen minutes.

2 Peel onions and chop them. Wash green chillies and slit them into two.

3 Heat oil in a kadai, add mustard seeds. When the mustard seeds crackle, add curry leaves and sauté for a few seconds. Add chopped onions and cook until soft and translucent.

4 Add ginger and garlic pastes, slit green chillies, turmeric powder and fish pieces. Cook on a high flame for half a minute.

5 Add coconut milk and salt and cook covered on a low flame for about ten minutes.

49

FISH
MOILEE

INGREDIENTS

Cumin seeds ....1 tspn

Coriander seeds ....2 tspns

Dried red chillies 4-5

Turmeric powder .... a pinch

Boneless fish .... 500 gms

Salt ....as per taste

Onions .... 2 medium sized

Grated coconut .... ¾ cup

Peppercorns 6-8

Tomato .... one medium sized

Oil .... 3 tblspns

Tamarind pulp .... 1 tblspn

METHOD OF PREPARATION

1 Lightly roast cumin seeds and coriander seeds. Grind them into a powder with dried red chillies and turmeric.

2 Cut boneless fish into one inch sized cubes. Apply salt. Apply ground chilli, turmeric, coriander and cumin masala.

3 Peel onions and chop one onion and grind the other onion with grated coconut, peppercorn into a coarse paste. Finely chop tomato and keep aside.

4 Heat oil in a pan, add chopped onions. Sauté till onions turn pink. Add chopped tomatoes and cook till oil leaves the sides.

5 Mix in ground coconut masala paste and cook on a high flame for a minute.

6 Add two cups of water and bring it to a boil. Add fish pieces and cook on medium flame for five to six minutes. Stir in tamarind dissolved in quarter cup of water. Simmer for five minutes.

7 Serve hot with steamed rice.

MALVANI FISH CURRY

PATRANI MACHCHI

INGREDIENTS

Pomfret fillets 8	Grated coconut ....½ cup
Salt .... as per taste	Cumin seeds .... 3 tspns
Lemon juice ....¼ cup	Garlic cloves 6-8
Coriander leaves ....1 cup	Banana leaves 3-4
Green chillies 4	

METHOD OF PREPARATION

1. Clean, wash and cut fish fillets into 2″ by 1 ½″ sized pieces
2. Sprinkle salt and half of the lemon juice and keep aside for half an hour.
3. Grind coriander leaves, green chillies, fresh grated coconut, cumin seeds and garlic to a fine paste. Add salt and lemon juice to it. Mix well.
4. Apply this marination to the fish fillets and keep for at least fifteen minutes.
5. Cut banana leaves into four pieces each.
6. Put marinated fish pieces in the banana leaves along with a little of the marination and fold the banana leaves to cover the fish fillets completely. Repeat the same with all the fish pieces.
7. Steam the fish in a steamer for fifteen minutes and serve hot.

PRAWN BALCHAO

INGREDIENTS

Shelled headless prawns ....600 gms
Ginger ....2 one inch pieces
Garlic .... 15-20 cloves
Cumin seeds ....1 tspn
Dry red chillies 12-15
Cloves 10-12
Cinnamon ....2 one inch sticks

Mustard seeds ....1 tspn
Malt vinegar ....1 cup
Onions ....2 large
Tomatoes ....4 large, red
Oil ....¾ cup
Sugar ....2 tblspns
Salt ....as per taste

METHOD OF PREPARATION

1. Devein the prawns. Wash and remove excess water. Add salt and keep aside. Peel and wash ginger.

2. Grind ginger, garlic, cumin seeds, dry red chillies, cloves, cinnamon and mustard seeds along with vinegar into a fine paste.

3. Peel onions and chop them finely. Wash and chop tomatoes.

4. Heat oil in a kadai and sauté the prawns till all the moisture dries up. Remove prawns and keep aside. In the same oil sauté onions till onions are soft and light brown. Add chopped tomatoes and cook on high heat till they form a thick pulp and oil leaves the masala.

5. Add the ground spices and stir fry for two to three minutes. Add the prawns and sugar. Check seasoning and cook on a low flame for another five to seven minutes till oil leaves the masala.

6. Serve hot with pav or boiled rice.

Chef's Tip: You need not use large sized prawns for this dish as Prawn balchao tastes better with small sized prawns and it is cheaper too !

INGREDIENTS

Shelled headless prawns ....400 gms

Cinnamon ....1 one inch stick

Cloves 8-10

Cumin seeds ....2 tspns

Coriander seeds ....1 tblspn

Whole red chillies 8-10

Grated coconut ....½ cup

Malt vinegar .... 2 tblspns

Onions .... 3 medium sized

Oil .... 3 tblspns

Ginger paste .... 1 tblspn

Garlic paste ....1 tblspn

Salt .... as per taste

METHOD OF PREPARATION

1 Wash and devein prawns.

2 Make a paste of cinnamon, cloves, cumin seeds, coriander seeds, whole red chillies and coconut with vinegar. Chop onions and keep aside.

3 Heat oil in a kadai. Add chopped onions and cook for about five minutes until light brown.

4 Add ginger paste, garlic paste and ground masala. Add ¾ cup water and cook on high flame for four to five minutes. Add prawns and salt and cook for five minutes on medium heat or till prawns are tender.

Chef's Tip: Do not overcook prawns as they tend to become tough on overcooking.

53

PRAWN
COCONUT
MASALA

TANDOORI POMFRET

INGREDIENTS

Pomfret fish ....2 (300 gram each)	Garlic paste .... 1 tblspn
Salt .... as per taste	Carom seeds (*ajwain*).......... ½ tspn
Lemon juice .... 2 tblspns	Gram flour (*besan*) .... 2 tblspns
Yogurt ....¾ cup	Turmeric powder ....½ tspn
Egg 1	Garam masala powder .... 1 tspn
Ginger paste .... 1 tblspn	Butter/oil .... 2 tblspns

METHOD OF PREPARATION

1 Wash and clean pomfret fish. Make incisions on it and apply salt and lemon juice. Keep aside for twenty minutes.

2 Mix all the other ingredients except butter/oil. Apply this marinade to the fish and let it stand for about one hour in the refrigerator.

3 Put the fish on a skewer and cook it in moderate hot tandoor or pre-heated oven (180 degree Celsius) for about eight to ten minutes.

4 Baste with butter and cook in tandoor/oven for another three minutes.

5 Serve hot with lemon wedges.

INGREDIENTS

Brinjal (*baingan*) ....1 kg	Cumin seeds ....1 tspn
Onions ....3 medium sized	Chopped ginger ....2 tspns
Tomatoes ....4 large sized	Red chilli powder .... 2 tspns
Green chillies 2	Salt .... as per taste
Oil ....3 tblspns	Chopped coriander leaves ......2 tblspns

METHOD OF PREPARATION

1 Prick brinjals and roast them over open flame or in a tandoor/pre-heated oven until skin starts peeling off and the brinjal starts to shrink. Let it cool. You can cool it by dipping it in water. Remove skin and mash it completely.

2 Peel onions and chop them. Wash tomatoes and chop them. Wash green chillies and chop them.

3 Heat oil in a kadai. Add cumin seeds. Cook for half a minute and add chopped onions and sauté until translucent. Then add chopped ginger, chopped green chillies and cook for half a minute.

4 Add red chilli powder and mashed roasted brinjals. Cook for seven to eight minutes over medium flame, stirring continuously. Add salt to taste.

5 Add chopped tomatoes and again cook on medium flame for seven to eight minutes till oil separates.

6 Garnish with chopped green coriander.

Chef's Tip: It is easy to remove skin of the roasted brinjal if it is dipped in water just after roasting. Use large sized round brinjals for this recipe. While buying, select brinjals that are light in weight in proportion to their size.

BAINGAN BHARTA

BEANS FOOGATH

INGREDIENTS

French beans .... 400 gms
Onions .... one large sized
Green chillies 2
Oil ....2 tblspns
Mustard seeds ....1 tspn
Curry leaves 8-10
Salt .... as per taste
Grated coconut ....½ cup
Lemon 1

METHOD OF PREPARATION

1 String and dice french beans finely. Peel onions and chop them. Wash green chillies and chop them.

2 Heat oil in a kadai, add mustard seeds and curry leaves. When mustard seeds begin to crackle, add chopped onions and green chillies. Stir on a high flame for a minute. Do not brown onion.

3 Add diced french beans and salt. Cook covered on a low flame for five to seven minutes or till beans are cooked but are still a little crunchy.

4 Add grated fresh coconut and juice of a lemon. Mix well and serve hot.

Chef's Tip: Do not overcook beans as they tend to lose colour and also the texture. This dish can be also enjoyed cold. After cooling, or if some of it is leftover, keep the beans foogath in the refrigerator and while serving, garnish with chopped onions, chopped green coriander and a little lemon juice.

Chicken bazarvi

Chicken chettinad

Shahi korma

BHINDI MASALA

INGREDIENTS

Lady finger (bhindi) .... 500 gms	Red chilli powder .... 1 tspn
Onions .... 2 large sized	Coriander powder .... 1 tblspn
Green chillies 3-4	Turmeric powder .... ½ tspn
Oil .... 4 tblspns	Dry mango powder (amchur) .... 2 tspns
Cumin seeds .... ½ tspn	Salt .... as per taste

METHOD OF PREPARATION

1. Peel and slice the onions. Wash green chillies and slit them into two.
2. Wash and dry the bhindi or wipe bhindi with a wet cloth. Cut both the ends and make 2″ long pieces. Slit bhindi horizontally without cutting them into two.
3. Heat oil in a kadai and add cumin seeds. Add onions and sauté till light golden. Add green chillies and sauté for half a minute.
4. Add bhindi and sprinkle the red chilli, coriander and turmeric powders over the bhindi. Mix well. Cook covered over low fire stirring occasionally. Add salt and amchur. When bhindi is almost cooked, finish cooking by cooking it on high flame for two minutes.

Chef's Tip : You may use tiny onions for this recipe. Peel and make deep cross cuts in onions and stuff with a mixture of turmeric powder, coriander powder, red chilli powder, salt and amchur. Use same stuffing for bhindi and cook covered, with a little oil and green chillies.

CORN CAPSICUM MASALA

INGREDIENTS

Corn kernels .... 300 gms
Capsicums .... 3 medium sized
Onions ....3 medium sized
Tomatoes ....2 medium sized
Coriander leaves .... ¼ cup
Oil .... 3 tblspns
Cumin seeds .... ½ tspn
Ginger paste .... 2 tblspns
Garlic paste .... 1 tblspn

Red chilli powder .... 1 tspn
Coriander powder .... 1 tblspn
Cumin powder .... 1 tspn
Turmeric powder .... ½ tspn
Mawa (khoya)...................... ½ cup
Garam masala powder ....1 tspn
Salt .... as per taste
Fresh cream (optional) ....¼ cup

METHOD OF PREPARATION

1 Boil corn in lots of water. Once cooked, drain out excess water and keep aside.

2 Wash, deseed and dice the capsicums into 1 cm sized cubes. Peel onions and chop them. Wash tomatoes and puree them in a mixer. Finely chop coriander leaves.

3 Heat oil in a kadai. Add cumin seeds, and when they begin to crackle, add chopped onions and sauté till golden brown.

4 Add ginger-garlic paste and cook for two to three minutes. Then add red chilli powder, coriander powder, cumin powder, and turmeric powder. Stir fry for a few seconds. Add chopped tomatoes and cook till oil leaves the masala, stirring continuously. Add mawa and half cup of water, mix well and cook for a minute.

5 Add diced capsicum and mix well. Finally add boiled corn, garam masala powder and salt. Mix and cook on low flame for four to five minutes.

6 Stir in fresh cream and chopped coriander leaves and serve hot.

Chef's Tip : This is a rich dish, to reduce calories go easy on mawa (khoya) and fresh cream. Use a little milk instead.

DUM KI ARBI

INGREDIENTS

Colocasia (*arbi*) ....700 gms	Green cardamom 4-6
Oil ....4 tblspns + for deep frying	Ginger paste .... 1 tblspn
Onions ....3 medium sized	Garlic paste ....1 tblspn
Poppy seeds (*khus khus*) ..... 3 tblspns	Coriander powder ....1 tspn
Yogurt ....2 cups	Grated nutmeg .... ¼ tspn
Red chilli powder ....½ tspn	Garam masala powder ....½ tspn
Turmeric powder ....½ tspn	Salt ....as per taste
Cumin powder ....1 tspn	Fresh cream ....¼ cup

METHOD OF PREPARATION

1. Peel and cut arbi into one inch sized pieces. Deep fry arbi in hot oil till crisp and golden brown.

2. Peel onions and cut into halves. Add two cups of water and boil till soft. Drain out excess water, cool and grind to a smooth paste.

3. Dry roast poppy seeds and then soak in water for half an hour. Grind to a smooth paste.

4. Whisk the yogurt along with red chilli powder, cumin powder and turmeric powder.

5. Heat oil in a pan. Add green cardamom, when they start to change colour slightly, add boiled onion paste. Sauté till light golden brown. Add ginger paste, garlic paste and coriander powder. Mix well. Stir in poppy seeds paste and cook for a minute.

6. Add the whisked yogurt, bring it to a boil. Add fried arbi, grated nutmeg, garam masala powder and salt.

7. Cover the pan with a tight-fitting lid and simmer for thirty minutes. Alternatively cover the pan with aluminium foil or seal the lid with wheat flour dough, so that the aroma is contained in the pan and does not escape.

8. Just before serving, open the lid and stir in fresh cream.

INGREDIENTS

For gattas

Gram flour *(besan)* .... 1 ½ cups
Yogurt .... 2 tblspns
Cumin .... ½ tspn
Red chilli powder .... ½ tspn
Chopped ginger .... ½ tspn
Chopped mint .... 1 tblspn
Turmeric powder .... ½ tspn
Salt .... as per taste
Soda bi-carbonate (baking soda)..... a pinch
Ghee/oil .... to deep fry
Garam masala powder .... ½ tspn

For gravy

Onion .... 2 medium sized
Yogurt .... 1 ½ cups
Red chilli powder .... 1 tspn
Coriander powder .... 2 tspns
Turmeric powder .... 1 tspn
Ghee/oil .... 2 tblspns
Cumin seeds .... 1 tspn
Cloves 4
Asafoetida .... a pinch
Salt .... as per taste

METHOD OF PREPARATION

1 Mix all the gatta ingredients except ghee/oil. Add two tblspns water to make a hard dough. Divide into six equal portions, roll into cylindrical shaped gattas.

2 Cook in two cups of boiling hot water for ten to fifteen minutes. Drain and reserve the water for the gravy. Cut the gattas into 1 inch pieces.

3 Heat ghee/oil and deep fry the gattas until light golden brown.

4 Peel onions and grate them. Mix yogurt, red chilli powder, coriander powder and turmeric powder.

5 Heat ghee/oil in a pan, add cumin seeds, cloves and asafoetida. Cook until cumin seeds start to change colour. Add grated onion, cook on high heat for three minutes till light pink.

6 Add yogurt mixed with spices. Cook on a low flame for five minutes.

7 Add gattas and then the water in which gattas were boiled. Cook on low flame until gravy is thick. Correct seasoning by adding salt and garam masala powder. Serve hot.

GATTA CURRY

INGREDIENTS

Cauliflower (small sized) 2	Cumin powder ....1 tspn
Salt ....as per taste	Red chilli powder .... 1 tblspn
Turmeric powder .... 1 tspn	Coriander powder ....1 tblspn
Onions ....2 medium sized	Garam masala powder ....1 tspn
Melon seeds .... ½ cup + 1 tspn	Tomato puree ....½ cup
Oil ....3 tblspns	Mawa (*khoya*).......................½ cup
Ginger paste .... 1 tblspn	Fresh cream .... ½ cup
Garlic paste ....1 tblspn	Chopped coriander leaves ....2 tblspns

METHOD OF PREPARATION

1 Remove stalks from cauliflower. Boil cauliflower in salted water with ½ tspn turmeric powder till half cooked. Peel onions and grate them. Soak ½ cup melon seeds in water for an hour and grind to a smooth paste.

2 Heat oil in a kadai. Add grated onions and sauté until golden brown in colour.

3 Add ginger paste, garlic paste, cumin powder, red chilli powder, coriander powder, remaining turmeric powder, garam masala powder and salt. Stir for half a minute.

4 Add tomato puree and cook till oil leaves the masala. Add melon seed paste dissolved in 1 cup of water. Bring to a boil. Add mawa. Mix well.

5 Add half-boiled cauliflower and cook covered on low heat or in a pre-heated oven for fifteen minutes. Top with fresh cream and simmer for five minutes.

6 Serve hot, garnished with chopped coriander leaves and melon seeds.

GOBHI
MUSSALLAM

KADAI VEGETABLES

INGREDIENTS

French beans	10-12	Green chillies	3-4
Carrots	2 medium sized	Ginger	1 two inch piece
Capsicums	2 medium sized	Coriander leaves	¼ cup
Cauliflower	¼ flower	Oil	4 tblspns
Tomatoes	3 large sized	Green peas	¼ cup
Onions	2 medium sized	Turmeric powder	½ tspn
Coriander seeds	1 tblspn	Coriander powder	1 tblspn
Cumin seeds	1 tspn	Red chilli powder	1 tspn
Dried red chillies	4-5	Salt	as per taste
Garlic	12-15 cloves	Garam masala powder	1 tspn

METHOD OF PREPARATION

1 String the beans and peel the carrots. Halve the capsicums and remove the seeds. Cut all the vegetables into ¼" cubes. Separate the cauliflower into small florets. Wash tomatoes and chop them roughly. Peel onions and slice them. Peel and wash ginger.

2 Grind coriander and cumin seeds and three red chillies coarsely.

3 Grind garlic, green chillies and half the ginger to a paste. Make julienne of the rest of the ginger. Finely chop the coriander leaves.

4 Heat oil in a pan. Add the coarsely ground masala. Add the sliced onions and sauté till golden brown.

5 Add ginger-garlic-green chilli paste and sauté for one minute. Add the vegetables except capsicum and stir. Cook covered on low heat till carrots are almost done. Sprinkle a little water if necessary.

6 Add turmeric powder, coriander powder and red chilli powder. Stir continuously. Add tomatoes, salt and half cup of water and cook till the vegetables are cooked and the water has dried up.

7 Add capsicum and salt, cook for four to five minutes on a low flame. Sprinkle garam masala powder.

8 Serve hot, garnished with ginger julienne and chopped coriander leaves.

KARELA MASALEDAAR

INGREDIENTS

Bitter gourd (*karela*) ...5-6 medium sized
Salt...................2 tblspns + as per taste
Oil ....3 tblspns + to fry
Onions ....2 medium sized

Turmeric powder ....1 tspn
Coriander powder .... 2 tspns
Dried mango powder (*amchur*)...1 tspn
Red chilli powder ....1 tspn

METHOD OF PREPARATION

1. Peel and reserve the scrapings of the karelas. Give a slit on one side and remove all the seeds. Cut karelas into thin slices. Wash and rub two table spoons salt all over the karelas and its scrapings. Set aside for three to four hours. Wash thoroughly again and squeeze dry the karelas.

2. Heat oil in kadai. Deep fry the sliced karelas till dark brown and crisp. Remove the karelas and keep aside.

3. Slice onions. Heat oil in a kadai. Add sliced onions. Sauté for three to four minutes till they are translucent. Add scrapings of karela and let it cook till onions are a little brown. Add turmeric powder, coriander powder, dry mango powder and red chilli powder.

4. Add the fried karelas to the above mixture and cook covered on low flame for five to six minutes.

5. Add salt if needed. Serve hot with chappatis.

Chef's Tip : Rubbing salt on karela takes out the bitterness to a great extent, be generous with salt while applying on the karela slices and later wash them thoroughly.

INGREDIENTS

Potatoes .... 18-20 small sized
Oil .... for deep-frying
Dried kashmiri chillies 5-6
Yogurt ....2 cups
Cardamom powder .... ½ tspn
Dry ginger powder .... 1 tspn
Fennel powder .... 2 tblspns

Mustard oil ....¼ cup
Clove powder .... a generous pinch
Asafoetida .... a pinch
Salt ....as per taste
Roasted cumin powder .... ½ tspn
Garam masala powder ....½ tspn

METHOD OF PREPARATION

1 Peel and prick the potatoes all over with the help of a fork. Keep in salted water for fifteen minutes. Heat oil in a kadai and fry the potatoes on medium flame till golden brown. Make a paste of dried Kashmiri red chillies.

2 Whisk the yogurt with Kashmiri red chilli paste, cardamom powder, dry ginger powder and fennel powder.

3 Heat mustard oil in a pan. Add clove powder and asafoetida. Add half a cup of water and salt and bring to a boil.

4 Stir in the yogurt mixture and bring it to a boil. Add fried potatoes and cook till the potatoes absorb the gravy and oil floats on top.

5 Serve hot, garnished with freshly roasted cumin powder and garam masala powder.

Chef's Tip: The process of pricking the potatoes makes them very light, if not, that means the pricking has not been proper or sufficient. Therefore it is a good idea to fry one potato and check. The size of the potato is also important, it should be of a small size but should not be very small.

Dum aloo served in most restaurants is very different from the recipe given here. However, I prefer this version.

64

KASHMIRI
DUM ALOO

MALAI KOFTA CURRY

INGREDIENTS

For koftas
Potatoes .... 4-5 medium sized
Cottage cheese (*paneer*) ....100 gms
Green chillies 2
Cornflour ....¼ cup
Salt ....as per taste
Raisins ....¼ cup
Oil ....for deep-frying
For gravy
Onions ....3 medium sized
Oil ....3 tblspns

Ginger paste ....1 tblspn
Garlic paste ....1 tblspn
Green chillies 2
Coriander powder ....1 tspn
Turmeric powder .... 1 tspn
Salt ....as per taste
Tomato puree ....½ cup
Red chilli powder ....1 tspn
Mawa (*khoya*).......................½ cup
Fresh cream ....½ cup
Garam masala powder .... 1 tspn

65

METHOD OF PREPARATION

1 Boil the potatoes, cool, peel and grate them. Grate paneer. Wash all green chillies, deseed and chop them fine. Peel onions, cut them into halves and boil with a cup of water for ten minutes. Drain excess water, cool onions and grind into a smooth paste.

2 Mix mashed potatoes, paneer, two chopped green chillies, cornflour and salt. Mix well. Divide into sixteen equal sized balls. Stuff raisins into them. Deep fry in hot oil until slightly coloured. Drain and keep aside.

3 Heat oil in a kadai. Add boiled onion paste and cook for five minutes. Add ginger paste, garlic paste, chopped green chillies, coriander powder, turmeric powder and salt.Cook for a minute. Add tomato puree and red chilli powder and cook on a medium flame for eight to ten minutes or till oil separates from the masala.

4 Mix mawa in two cups of water and add to the gravy. Bring it to a boil and simmer for ten minutes on a slow flame. Stir occasionally. Stir in fresh cream and garam masala powder.

5 Place warm koftas in a serving dish and pour hot gravy on top and serve.

Chef's Tip : Fry one kofta and check for binding, if it breaks, add a little more cornflour. Deep fry in hot oil.

INGREDIENTS

Shelled green peas	1 ½ cups	Tomato puree	½ cup
Mushrooms	200 gms	Red chilli powder	1 tblspn
Oil	2 tblspns	Coriander powder	1 tblspn
Green cardamom	4	Turmeric powder	1 tspn
Cinnamon	1 one inch stick	Garam masala powder	1 tspn
Onions	2 large sized	Salt	as per taste
Ginger paste	1 tblspn	Cashewnut paste	½ cup
Garlic paste	1 tblspn		

METHOD OF PREPARATION

1. Clean, wash and cut mushrooms in quarters. Peel onions and chop them finely.

2. Heat oil in a kadai. Add green cardamom, cinnamon stick and chopped onions and sauté until light golden brown.

3. Add ginger paste, garlic paste, and cook for half a minute. Add tomato puree, red chilli powder, coriander powder, turmeric powder, garam masala powder and salt and cook till oil leaves the masala.

4. Add cashewnut paste dissolved in one cup of water, stir well. Add a cup of water, bring it to a boil and then add green peas and mushrooms. Cook on high flame for seven to eight minutes or till green peas are fully cooked.

5. Cook on a low flame for five minutes. Serve hot.

MATAR MUSHROOM

METHI KELA BHAJI

INGREDIENTS

Fenugreek leaves (*methi*) ......3 cups
Ripe bananas 3-4
Ginger ....2 one inch pieces
Green chillies 3-4
Turmeric powder ....½ tspn

Coriander powder ....2 tsps
Cumin powder ....2 tspns
Oil ....4 tblspns
Mustard seeds ....½ tspn
Salt ....as per taste

METHOD OF PREPARATION

1   Separate the methi leaves from stems. Wash thoroughly under running water. Chop finely and keep aside.

2   Cut bananas into one inch thick roundels with their skin on. Peel ginger and wash green chillies. Make a paste of ginger and green chillies.

3   Heat oil in a kadai. Add mustard seeds. When they start to crackle, add the chopped methi leaves and salt. Cook for ten to fifteen minutes on medium heat. Add turmeric powder and mix. Add ginger-green chilli paste, stir fry for a minute. Add coriander and cumin powder. Mix well. Cook for one to two minutes.

4   Finally add the banana roundels. Correct seasoning. Cook covered on low heat for two minutes.

5   Serve hot with chappatis/rotis of your choice.

INGREDIENTS

Fenugreek leaves (*methi*) .... 2 cups
Shelled green peas .... 1 cup
Onions .... 2 medium sized
Ginger paste ....1 tblspn
Garlic paste ....1 tblspn
Green chillies 3
Chopped coriander leaves .... 2 tblspns
Fresh corn kernels ....1 cup
Lemon juice ....1 tblspn

Yogurt ....½ cup
Turmeric powder .... a pinch
Red chilli powder .... 1 tspn
Oil ....2 tblspns
Cumin seeds ....1 tspn
Mawa (*khoya*) .... ½ cup
Salt ....as per taste
Fresh cream ....1 cup

METHOD OF PREPARATION

1 Peel onions and grate them. Wash green chillies and chop them fine. Set aside.

2 Clean the methi leaves, wash them thoroughly and chop. Add one tea spoon salt and set aside for half an hour. Squeeze dry and wash again.

3 Boil the corn in water with lemon juice till soft. Drain and keep aside. Wash the peas and boil in water. Drain and keep aside. Whisk the yogurt with turmeric and red chilli powders. Mash mawa and keep aside.

4 Heat oil in a pan. Add cumin seeds. When they start to change colour, add grated onions and cook till brown, stirring continuously. Add ginger and garlic pastes and continue to cook. Add chopped methi leaves and chopped green chillies. Cook till all the moisture dries up.

5 Add the yogurt mixture and cook till oil separates. Now add cooked corn and green peas. Add mashed mawa and one cup of water. Add salt to taste. Cook for ten minutes.

6 Stir in fresh cream and mix well. Simmer for five minutes. Serve hot with chopped coriander leaves.

METHI MATAR MAKAI

INGREDIENTS

Green chillies (large) 18-20
Oil ....2 tblspns + to fry chillies
Sesame seeds .... 2 tblspns
Roasted peanuts .... ½ cup
Mustard seeds ....1 tspn
Coriander seeds .... 1 tblspn
Cumin seeds .... 1 tspn
Dry red chillies 2

Turmeric powder ....1 tspn
Onion ....1 medium sized
Ginger ....1 one inch piece
Garlic ....6-8 cloves
Curry leaves 8-10
Tamarind pulp ....2 tblspns
Salt .... as per taste

METHOD OF PREPARATION

1. Wash, wipe and slit green chillies lengthwise without cutting the chillies into two. Deep fry in hot oil for one minute. Remove on a paper towel and keep aside.

2. Peel and grate onion. Peel ginger and roughly chop. Dry roast sesame seeds, coriander seeds and cumin seeds. Make a paste of roasted sesame seeds, roasted peanuts, coriander seeds, cumin seeds, dry red chillies, ginger and garlic cloves.

3. Heat oil in a pan, add mustard seeds, let it crackle and add curry leaves. Now, add grated onion. Sauté until onion is light golden brown. Make sure to stir continuously.

4. Add turmeric powder and mix well. Add masala paste and cook for three minutes, stirring constantly. Stir in one and half cups of water and bring it to a boil. Reduce the heat and cook for ten minutes. Add tamarind pulp (dissolved in half a cup of water, if it is too thick).

5. Add fried green chillies and salt and cook on low heat for eight to ten minutes.

In Hyderabad, Mirchi ka salan is traditionally served as an accompaniment to biryanis. Some people like to add grated coconut to the masala paste, but I prefer Mirchi ka salan without coconut. This gravy is referred to as Tili (Til - Sesame) aur Falli (Moong falli - Peanuts) gravy.

INGREDIENTS

Potatoes	2 medium sized	Cumin seeds	1 tspn
Broad beans (papdi)	12-15	Coriander seeds	1 tblspn
Shelled green peas	½ cup	Garlic cloves	8-10
Cauliflower	¼ flower	Turmeric powder	1 tspn
Carrots	2 medium sized	Salt	as per taste
Red pumpkin	100 gms	Groundnut oil	3 tblspns
Grated coconut	1 ½ cups	Mustard seeds	1 tspn
Tamarind pulp	2 tblspns	Split black gram (urad dal, dhuli)	1 tspn
Dried red chillies	4	Curry leaves	8-10

METHOD OF PREPARATION

1   Peel and dice the potatoes into 1   cubes. String the beans, halve them and cut them into one inch sized pieces. Wash cauliflower and separate the cauliflower florets. Peel and dice the carrots into 1   cubes. Peel and dice the pumpkin into 1 cubes.

2   Add warm water to one cup of grated coconut and extract thick and thin milk. Keep aside. Dissolve tamarind pulp in half cup of water.

3   Heat a little oil and sauté two dried red chillies, cumin seeds, coriander seeds, garlic and the remaining half cup of grated coconut till a nice aroma is given out. Grind into a fine paste with a little water.

4   Boil the vegetables in the thin coconut milk with turmeric powder, tamarind extract and salt till three-fourths done. Add the ground masala and cook for ten minutes.

5   Heat a little oil separately and add the remaining red chillies broken into two, mustard seeds and urad dal. Add curry leaves and add this to the vegetables.

6   Continue cooking the vegetables till done. Then add the thick coconut milk and simmer for two to three minutes. Serve hot with boiled rice.

Chef's Tip : If broad beans are not available replace them with french beans.

MIXED VEGETABLES IN COCONUT MILK

INGREDIENTS

Spinach ....2 large bunches (900 gms)
Cottage cheese (*paneer*) .... 200 gms
Garlic ....8-10 cloves
Green chillies 2-3
Oil .... 3 tblspns

Cumin seeds ....½ tspn
Salt .... as per taste
Lemon juice ....1 tblspn
Fresh cream ....4 tblspns

METHOD OF PREPARATION

1 Remove stems and wash spinach thoroughly under running water. Blanch in salted boiling water for two minutes. Refresh in chilled water. Squeeze out excess water. Grind into a fine paste along with green chillies.

2 Dice the paneer into 1"x 1"x ½" pieces. Chop garlic and keep aside.

3 Heat oil in a pan. Add cumin seeds. When they begin to change colour, add chopped garlic and sauté for half a minute. Add the spinach puree and stir. Check seasoning. Add water if required.

4 When the gravy comes to a boil, add the paneer dices and mix well. Stir in lemon juice. Finally add fresh cream.

5 Serve hot.

Chef's Tip: Palak paneer tastes best without too many spices and herbs. To get best results, do not overcook spinach, as overcooking would not only adversely affect the bright green colour of spinach but also the taste.

PALAK PANEER

PANEER JHALFRAIZEE

INGREDIENTS

Dry red chillies 2
Onions ....2 medium sized
Ginger .... 2 one inch pieces
Green chillies 1-2
Tomatoes ....2 medium sized
Capsicums .... 2 medium sized
Cottage cheese (paneer) ....400 gms
Coriander leaves ....¼ cup

Oil ....3 tblspns
Cumin seeds ....1 tspn
Red chilli powder .... 1 ½ tspns
Turmeric powder ....1 tspn
Vinegar .... 1 ½ tblspns
Salt .... as per taste
Garam masala powder ....1 tspn

METHOD OF PREPARATION

1 Break the red chillies into two pieces.

2 Peel onions and cut into thick slices, separate the different layers of onion. Peel ginger and cut into julienne. Wash green chillies and chop them.

3 Cut the tomatoes and capsicums into half, remove the seeds and cut them into long slices with half centimetre width. Finely chop the coriander leaves. Cut the paneer into finger sized pieces.

4 Heat oil in a kadai. Add cumin seeds. When they start to change colour, add the halved red chillies. Add ginger julienne and sliced onions. Sauté for half a minute.

5 Add red chilli powder and turmeric powder. Stir well and then mix capsicum pieces and cook for two to three minutes. Add paneer fingers and toss. Add salt and vinegar and cook for two to three minutes. Stir in tomato pieces and garam masala powder.

6 Serve hot, garnished with chopped coriander leaves.

Paneer jhalfraizee

Goli biryani, Lemon rice, Mutton Biryani

Jalebi, Chocolate burfi, Besan ke laddoo

SHAAM SAVERA

INGREDIENTS

For kofta

Spinach	600 gms
Green chillies	3-4
Garlic	6-8 cloves
Cornflour (cornstarch)	3 tblspns
Salt	as per taste
Oil	to deep fry
Cottage cheese (paneer)	125 gms

For tomato gravy

Butter	3 tblspns
Whole garam masala	1 tblspn
Ginger paste	1 tblspn
Garlic paste	1 tblspn
Tomato puree	2 cups
Red chilli powder	1 tblspn
Garam masala powder	½ tspn
Sugar/honey	3 tblspns
Dried fenugreek leaves, crushed (kasoori methi)	½ tspn
Fresh cream	1 cup
Chopped coriander leaves	2 tblspns
Salt	as per taste

METHOD OF PREPARATION

1 Wash spinach under plenty of running water to get rid of any dirt. Blanch in boiling hot water and refresh in cold water. Squeeze out water and finely chop the spinach and also green chillies. Add half of chopped green chillies, salt, chopped garlic and cornflour to chopped spinach. Mix well and divide into twelve equal portions.

2 Grate paneer. Add salt and mash well. Divide into twelve equal balls.

3 Take spinach portions, flatten them on your palm and stuff paneer balls in them. Shape into balls. Deep fry in moderately hot oil for five minutes. Drain and keep aside.

4 Heat butter in a pan, add whole garam masala. When they crackle, add ginger-garlic paste and remaining chopped green chillies. Cook for two minutes.

5 Add tomato puree, red chilli powder, garam masala powder, salt and one cup of water. Bring it to a boil, reduce heat and simmer for ten minutes. Add sugar or honey and kasoori methi. Stir in fresh cream.

6 Serve koftas cut into halves on top of tomato gravy. Do not boil koftas in the gravy as they may break.

Chef's Tip : Before proceeding with all the koftas, deep fry one and check if they are breaking. If yes, add some more cornstarch in the spinach mixture and then deep fry in hot oil. Whole garam masala for this recipe consists of 4 green cardamon, 6 cloves and a bayleaf.

SOYABEAN GRANULES SABZI

INGREDIENTS

Onions	3 medium sized	Oil	3 tblspns
Tomatoes	3 medium sized	Cumin seeds	1 tspn
Ginger	1 two inch piece	Milk	3 cups
Green chillies	2	Red chilli powder	1 tspn
Soyabean granules	200 gms	Turmeric powder	½ tspn
Coriander leaves	¼ cup	Salt	as per taste

METHOD OF PREPARATION

1. Peel and finely chop the onions. Peel ginger, wash green chillies and make a paste of ginger and green chillies. Thoroughly wash coriander leaves and finely chop them. Wash and chop tomatoes.

2. Wash soyabean granules with lukewarm water. Drain and then soak in warm milk for half an hour.

3. Heat oil in a pan. Add cumin seeds. When they start to change colour, add chopped onions and fry till light golden brown. Add ginger, green chilli paste and cook for half a minute.

4. Add chopped tomatoes and cook for four to five minutes. Add red chilli powder and turmeric powder. Cook till oil leaves the masala.

5. Add the soyabean granules and mix well. Cook covered till soya granules are cooked. This normally takes about ten minutes. Add a little water if required. Add salt and cook till it is almost dry.

6. Serve hot, garnished with chopped coriander leaves.

INGREDIENTS

Small sized potatoes	6-8	Mustard seeds	1 tspn
Yam *(kand)*	100 gms	Salt	as per taste
Raw bananas	2	Turmeric powder	1 tspn
Small brinjals	3-4	**For muthiya**	
Broad beans *(papdi)*	25-30	Gram flour *(besan)*	¼ cup
Garlic	6-8 cloves	Salt	as per taste
Green chillies	4	Fenugreek leaves	½ cup
Ginger	2 one inch pieces	Ginger	1 half inch piece
Coriander leaves	1 cup	Green chillies	1-2
Oil	5 tblspns	Oil	to deep fry
Asafoetida	a pinch		

METHOD OF PREPARATION

1. Wash, peel and dice potatoes, yam and raw bananas. Wash and chop coriander leaves.
2. Wash brinjals and slit them into four without cutting the stem.
3. Make a paste of garlic, green chilli and ginger. Mix chopped coriander to the paste.
4. Mix all the muthiya ingredients except oil and prepare a stiff dough by using a little water. Divide into small portions and shape each into one inch long, half inch thick rolls. Deep fry in hot oil, till golden brown. Drain and keep aside.
5. String beans and cut into one inch long pieces.
6. Heat oil in a thick bottomed handi, add asafoetida and mustard seeds. When mustard seeds crackle, add ground masala and broad beans. Mix well. Place the rest of the vegetables in layers one on top of the other (interspread with masala and broad beans). Sprinkle salt and turmeric powder. Cook for five minutes on high flame.
7. Pour one cup of water, cover and simmer on a very low flame for ten to fifteen minutes.
8. Add fried muthiyas and again simmer for fifteen minutes. Shake the vegetables occasionally but do not use a spoon to stir.
9. Serve hot, garnished with grated coconut.

Chef's Tip : Traditionally Undhiyo is served with a lot of oil floating on top. You may vary the quantity of oil used as per your taste. Use surati papdi, (a special variety of broad beans) and purple kand (yam) for this recipe for best results.

UNDHIYO

BEETROOT RAITA

INGREDIENTS

Beetroots .... 2 medium sized
Yogurt .... 3 cups
Roasted cumin powder ....1 tspn

Red chilli powder ....1 tspn
Salt .... as per taste

METHOD OF PREPARATION

1 Boil beetroot. Peel, cool and dice into half centimeter sized pieces. Keep aside.

2 Beat yogurt to a smooth consistency. You can also strain the yogurt through a muslin cloth to get a smooth consistency.

3 Mix chopped beetroots with yogurt. Add roasted cumin powder, red chilli powder and salt.

4 Mix well and serve chilled.

Chef's Tip : The bright and dark colour of beetroot will bleed and change the colour of the yogurt to dark pink. Plan the rest of your meal accordingly.

INGREDIENTS

White gram, split *(urad dal)*....2 cups
Cumin seeds ....1 tspn
Fennel seeds *(saunf)* .... ½ tspn
Cashewnuts 15-20
Raisins ....2 tblspns
Black pepper corns .... ½ tspn
Salt .... as per taste

Oil ....to fry
Yogurt .... 6 cups
Roasted cumin powder .... 1 tspn
Red chilli powder ....1 tspn
Chopped coriander leaves ..... for garnish
Ginger julienne .... for garnish
Tamarind chutney ... as accompaniment

METHOD OF PREPARATION

1 Soak urad dal in enough water for six hours. Grind to a paste; the batter should be thick, not runny. Add cumin seeds, saunf and salt and mix well. Chop cashewnuts and raisins. Mix well.

2 Heat oil in a kadai. Pour a small ladle full of dal batter on a plastic sheet of 6"x 6". Spread the batter into a circle of 2 ½ diametre. Place a teaspoon of cashewnut and raisin stuffing in the center. Hold two top corners of the plastic sheet and bring towards you to join them with the other two corners. This will fold the batter into crescent shape. Gently slide the gujia into hot oil.

3 Deep fry the gujias till golden brown. Soak in warm water.

4 Beat yogurt to a smooth consistency, add salt.

5 Squeeze the gujias and put in the yogurt.

6 Sprinkle roasted cumin powder, red chilli powder, chopped coriander leaves and ginger julienne before serving.

7 Serve topped with tamarind chutney.

Chef's Tip : I have seen my mother use milk poly-bags instead of plastic sheets. The thickness of these bags is just right for this purpose. However cut open the bag and wash before use.

DAHI GUJIA

DAHI VADA

INGREDIENTS

White gram, split *(urad dal)* .... 1 cup
Cumin seeds .... 1 tspn
Salt ....as per taste
Asafoetida .... a pinch
Oil ....for deep frying

Yogurt .... 3 cups
Roasted cumin powder ....1 tspn
Red chilli powder ....1 tspn
Chopped green coriander ....1 tblspn

METHOD OF PREPARATION

1 Pick, wash and soak dal in two cups of water for six to eight hours.
2 Drain and grind into a fine and fluffy paste. Add cumin seeds, salt and asafoetida and then whisk the mixture to incorporate air into it.
3 Heat oil in a kadai to moderate heat. Take about two tblspns of dal mixture on your wet palm and make a hole in the centre with your thumb, shape like a doughnut and lower into the hot oil. Deep fry the vadas till golden brown.
4 Drain and soak in warm water.
5 Beat yogurt with a whisk to make it smooth. Add salt and mix well.
6 Squeeze the vadas to remove excess water and add into the yogurt. Let them soak for at least fifteen to twenty minutes before serving.
7 Garnish with roasted cumin powder, red chilli powder and chopped coriander. Serve cold.

Chef's Tip : You may top it with tamarind chutney.

INGREDIENTS

Black gram, whole *(urad)* ...... 1 cup
Salt .... as per taste
Ginger paste .... 2 tblspns
Garlic paste .... 2 tblspns
Red chilli powder .... 1 tblspn

Butter .... 100 gms
Fresh Cream .... 1 cup
Tomato puree .... 1 ½ cups
Garam masala powder .... 2 tspns

METHOD OF PREPARATION

1. Pick and wash whole black urad. Soak it in four cups of water for eight to ten hours or overnight.

2. Cook it in four to five cups of water along with salt, red chilli powder and ginger paste. Bring it to a boil. Reduce flame and simmer for about an hour or till it is completely cooked and tender.

3. Melt butter in a thick bottomed pan and add garlic paste dissolved in half a cup of water. Cook for two minutes, stirring constantly.

4. Add tomato puree, butter and garam masala powder, add cooked dal to this and cook on a low flame for an hour. Stir occasionally. Add water if required.

5. Add fresh cream, correct seasoning and simmer for another ten minutes. The consistency of this dal is quite thick.

6. Serve hot with bread of your choice.

Chef Kapoor enjoys it with Pudina parantha!

79

DAL
PAKHTOONI

LAUKI RAITA

INGREDIENTS

Bottlegourd *(lauki/doodhi)* .....250 gms

Salt .... as per taste

Yogurt, chilled........................ 3 cups

Cumin seeds .... 1 tspn

Red chilli powder .... ½ tspn

METHOD OF PREPARATION

1 Peel, wash and grate lauki. Boil grated lauki with a little salt for five minutes. Drain out water and cool grated lauki.

2 Whisk chilled yogurt and mix salt and red chilli powder. Add cooked lauki and mix well.

3 Dry roast cumin seeds and make a coarse powder. Serve lauki raita topped with cumin powder.

Chef's Tip : Ensure to squeeze out excess water from cooked lauki.

MASALEDAAR CHHOLAY

INGREDIENTS

Chick peas (kabuli chana)........ 1 ½ cups
Salt .... as per taste
Tea leaves ....2 tspns
Dried Indian gooseberry (amla)..... 3-4
Onions .... 3 large sized
Ginger ....2 one inch pieces
Garlic ....8-10 cloves
Green chillies 2

Tomatoes ....4 medium sized
Coriander leaves ....¼ cup
Oil .... 4 tblspns
Cumin seeds ....2 tblspns
Coriander powder ....3 tspns
Red chilli powder ....1 tspn
Pomegranate seeds (anardana) powder (coarse) ....1 tblspn

METHOD OF PREPARATION:

1   Soak the chana overnight in water. Boil in the same water with salt, dried amla and tea leaves (tied in a piece of muslin cloth) till tender. Remove amla and tea leaves.

2   Peel and chop the onions. Peel ginger and garlic. Wash green chillies and make a paste of ginger, garlic and green chillies. Wash and chop the tomatoes and coriander leaves. Dry roast cumin seeds, cool and grind to a powder.

3   Heat oil in a pan, add chopped onions and sauté till brown. Add ginger-garlic-green chilli paste and sauté for sometime.

4   Add coriander powder, ground roasted cumin seeds, red chilli, turmeric and anardana powders and cook till oil separates.

5   Add drained chana and mix well. Add tomatoes and a little cooking liquor and salt if required. Cook till the chanas are well mixed with the gravy.

6   Serve hot, garnished with coriander leaves.

Chef's Tip : If you like, you may add boiled and diced potatoes.

INGREDIENTS

Split green gram *(moong dal, dhuli)* ...¾ cup
Salt .... as per taste
Turmeric powder .... 1 tspn
Spinach ....15-20 leaves
Oil ....2 tblspns
Asafoetida .... a pinch

Cumin seeds .... 1 tspn
Onions ....2 medium sized
Green chillies 2
Ginger .... 1 one inch piece
Garlic .... 6-8 cloves
Lemon juice .... 1 tspn

METHOD OF PREPARATION

1 Pick, wash and boil moong dal with salt and turmeric powder in five cups of water. Cook till dal is fully cooked.

2 Wash spinach leaves thoroughly under cold running water. Then roughly shred them. Peel onions and chop them finely. Wash green chillies, deseed and chop them finely. Peel and chop garlic, keep aside. Wash and chop ginger.

3 Heat oil in a kadai. Add asafoetida and cumin seeds. When cumin seeds start to change colour, add chopped onions and chopped green chillies. Cook till onions are soft and translucent.

4 Add chopped ginger and garlic, cook for half a minute.

5 Add the boiled dal. Bring to a boil and add shredded spinach and lemon juice.

6 Simmer for two minutes and serve hot.

82

PALAK WALI DAL

INGREDIENTS

Split gram *(chana dal)* .... ¼ cup
Whole green gram *(moong)* .... ¼ cup
Split black gram, skinless *(urad dal)* ..... ¼ cup
Pigeon peas, split *(toor dal)* .... ¼ cup
Red lentils *(masoor)* .... ¼ cup
Salt .... as per taste
Ginger .... 1 one inch piece
Dried red chillies 2
Coriander powder .... 1 tspn
Green chillies 2

Coriander leaves .... 2 tblspns
Cumin powder .... 1 tspn
Red chilli powder .... ½ tspn
Turmeric powder .... ½ tspn
Tomatoes .... 2 medium sized
Oil .... 3 tblspns
Cumin seeds .... ½ tspn
Cloves 4-5
Asafoetida .... a pinch
Garam masala powder .... ½ tspn

METHOD OF PREPARATION

1 Soak the pulses for at least two hours. Then boil them in salted water with turmeric powder till done. Wash green chillies, coriander leaves and peel ginger.

2 Make a paste of ginger and green chillies. Chop the coriander leaves. Wash and chop the tomatoes.

3 Heat oil in a pan. Add asafoetida, cumin seeds, cloves and dried red chillies. When cumin starts to change colour, add ginger-green chilli paste and sauté for sometime.

4 Add cumin powder, coriander powder and red chilli powder. Add the tomatoes and cook till oil separates. Add cooked lentils and water if required.

5 Cook for ten minutes, stirring well. Add garam masala powder and serve hot.

83

RAJASTHANI
PANCHMEL
DAL

INGREDIENTS

Red kidney beans *(rajma)* ..... 1 ½ cups
Oil ....3 tblspns
Bay leaves 2
Onions ....2 medium sized
Ginger .... 1 one inch piece
Garlic ....6-8 cloves
Red chilli powder ....2 tspns

Coriander powder ....1 tblspn
Turmeric powder ....½ tspn
Cumin powder ....1 tspn
Tomatoes ....3 medium sized
Garam masala powder ....1 tspn
Chopped fresh coriander ....1 tblspn
Salt .... as per taste

METHOD OF PREPARATION

1. Soak rajma overnight in five cups of water.
2. Boil rajma or pressure cook till fully cooked and soft. Wash and peel ginger. Chop it finely. Chop garlic. Wash and chop tomatoes and peel and chop onions.
3. Heat oil, add bay leaves, chopped onions and sauté till onions are golden brown in colour. Add chopped ginger and garlic and cook for a minute.
4. Add red chilli powder, coriander powder, turmeric powder, cumin powder and stir. Add chopped tomatoes and cook till tomatoes are cooked and oil leaves the masala.
5. Add boiled rajma along with its cooking liquor and cook on a low flame for fifteen minutes, stirring in between. Add garam masala powder and cook for five minutes. Garnish with chopped fresh coriander. Serve hot with steamed rice.

In my mother's house, Mothi (Rajma) - Chawal has always been a Sunday lunch treat, week after week, month after month, year after year....!

84

RAJMA
RASMISA

SOOKHI MOONG DAL

INGREDIENTS

Split green gram skinless (moong dal, dhuli) .... 1 ¼ cups	Oil .... 3 tblspns
Salt .... as per taste	Cumin seeds .... ½ tspn
Ginger .... 2 one inch pieces	Asafoetida .... a pinch
Green chilli 1	Red chilli powder .... 1 tspn
Chopped coriander leaves .... 1 tblspn	Turmeric powder .... ½ tspn
	Lemon juice .... 2 tspns

METHOD OF PREPARATION

1. Wash and soak the moong dal in water for half an hour. Boil dal with salt and turmeric powder till it is just cooked but not mashed.
2. Drain excess water, if any.
3. Peel ginger and wash green chilli. Chop ginger and green chilli.
4. Heat oil in a kadai. Add cumin seeds and asafoetida. Once the cumin seeds start to change colour, add chopped ginger and green chilli and sauté for half a minute.
5. Add red chilli powder and cooked dal. Mix and season with lemon juice and salt if required. Mix lightly, taking care not to mash the cooked dal and cook till dry.
6. Serve hot, garnished with chopped coriander leaves.

ANDA PARANTHA

INGREDIENTS

Flour (maida)	1 cup	Eggs	5
Wheat flour (atta)	1 cup	Carom seeds (ajwain)	½ tspn
Salt	as per taste	Butter	2 tblspns
Green chillies	2	Oil	5 tblspns
Coriander leaves	¼ cup		

METHOD OF PREPARATION

1. Sieve maida, atta and one tea spoon salt together.
2. Wash green chillies. Finely chop them. Wash and finely chop coriander leaves.
3. Break four eggs and whisk with salt.
4. Make a soft dough with atta, maida, salt, green chillies, ajwain, one egg and water (approx. ¾ cup). Cover with a moist cloth and set aside for an hour.
5. Divide the dough into four equal parts. Roll out each into 4" diameter disc. Spread a little butter on each disc, sprinkle a little wheat flour and fold into four.
6. Roll out again on floured surface into 6" sized triangular parantha.
7. Place over a heated tawa. When one side is half done, turn over and spread some egg and coriander leaves on the upper side. Apply oil around the edges and turn over.
8. Apply some egg and coriander leaves on the other side and shallow fry till both sides are evenly golden brown.
9. Serve hot with pickle of your choice.

INGREDIENTS

Refined flour *(maida)* .... 2 ½ cups	Salt ....1 tspn
Yogurt ....½ cup	Sugar ....2 tspns
Baking powder ....½ tspn	Oil ....2 tblspns + for frying
Soda bi-carbonate (baking soda) .... a pinch	

METHOD OF PREPARATION

1 Take flour and add baking powder, soda bi-carbonate and salt. Mix well and pass it through a sieve.

2 Mix yogurt and sugar. Add this to the flour and add about a cup of water and mix gradually to make a soft dough by light kneading.

3 Incorporate two tblspns oil into the dough and cover the dough with a wet cloth. Keep it aside for an hour.

4 Divide it into sixteen equal portions, roll them into balls. Cover and keep to ferment for ten minutes.

5 Grease your palms with a little oil and flatten the balls. Roll into five inch diameter diskettes.

6 Heat oil in a kadai and deep fry bhaturas on high flame till light brown on both sides.

Chef's Tip: You can make bhaturas of oval shape by pulling the rolled diskettes from opposite sides.

BHATURA

CHAWAL KA PARANTHA

INGREDIENTS

Whole wheat flour *(atta)* ..... 1 ¼ cups	Steamed rice .... 1 cup
Salt .... 1 tspn	Red chilli powder .... ½ tspn
Yogurt .... ¼ cup	Cumin powder .... ½ tspn
Ghee .... 2 tblspns	Green chillies 2
Onion .... 1 medium sized	Oil .... to cook parantha

88

METHOD OF PREPARATION

1. Sieve whole wheat flour along with salt. Make a soft dough with yogurt, two tablespoons ghee and half cup of water. Cover with a moist cloth and set aside for half an hour.
2. Knead again and divide into four equal parts. Make balls and press between palms of your hand to make pedhas.
3. Peel and chop onion finely. Wash and chop green chillies.
4. Mix cooked rice with red chilli powder, cumin powder, chopped green chillies, chopped onions and salt.
5. Roll out each pedha into 3″ diameter disc.
6. Stuff rice mixture in the flattened pedha and shape into a pedha again.
7. Roll out into a 7″ diameter disc using a rolling pin.
8. Heat a tawa. Place the parantha over it. Turn over once and spread some oil around it. Turn over again and spread a little more oil on the other side. Cook till both sides are well cooked.
9. Serve hot with fresh yogurt and pickle of your choice.

Chef's Tip : You can use leftover rice for this recipe and the rice need not be reheated. It can be used straight out of the refrigerator.

Malai ki kheer, Gulab jamun, Rasmalai

Doi machhi

CHICKEN PULAO

INGREDIENTS

Basmati rice ....2 cups	Cumin seeds ....1 tspn
Chicken (boneless)............600 gms	Cloves 6-8
Onions ....2 medium sized	Cinnamon ....2 one inch sticks
Tomatoes ....3 medium sized	Green cardamom 6-8
Ginger paste ....2 tblspns	Bay leaves 2
Garlic paste ....2 tblspns	Red chilli powder ....1 tspn
Salt.............................. as per taste	Chicken stock ....3 ½ cups
Ghee ....4 tblspns	Yogurt ....½ cup

METHOD OF PREPARATION

1 Peel and slice the onions. Wash tomatoes and chop them finely. Cut boneless chicken into 1 ½" sized pieces.

2 Marinate the chicken in yogurt, ginger and garlic pastes and salt for an hour.

3 Clean, wash and soak the rice for an hour. Drain and keep aside.

4 Heat ghee in a thick-bottomed pan. Add cumin seeds. Stir fry for ten seconds. Add cloves, green cardamom, cinnamon sticks and bay leaves. Stir fry again for about ten seconds.

5 Add sliced onions and sauté till golden brown. Add chopped tomatoes and cook on high heat for three minutes, stirring continuously. Mix in red chilli powder.

6 Add chicken along with the marinade and sauté till the chicken is half cooked. Add stock and bring to a boil.

7 Stir in rice and bring it to a boil and then lower the heat. Cook till the water level reaches the rice level.

8 Cover the rice with a lid and cook on low heat for twenty minutes or till rice and chicken are fully cooked. Remove the lid and separate the rice granules so that rice does not form lumps.

9 Serve along with raita and kachumber.

Chef's Tip: You can also cook Chicken pulao by using chicken pieces with bones.

89

GOLI BIRYANI

INGREDIENTS

Chicken bones	1 kg	Chicken mince	600 gms
Basmati rice	1 ½ cups	Salt	as per taste
Bay leaves	2	Ghee	½ cups
Ginger	2 one inch pieces	Cumin seeds	1 tspn
Green chillies	3-4	Mace	2 blades
Coriander leaves	¼ cup	Green cardamom	6-8
Mint leaves	¼ cup	Cloves	6-8
Garlic	6-8 cloves	Coriander powder	2 tblspns
Onions	2 medium sized	Saffron	a generous pinch
Yogurt	1 ½ cups	Milk	½ cup
Red chilli powder	1 tspn	Garam masala powder	2 tspns
Turmeric powder	½ tspn		

METHOD OF PREPARATION

1 Wash and boil the chicken bones in 1½ litres of water for twenty minutes. Drain and keep aside. Discard bones.

2 Wash and soak the rice in water for thirty minutes. Boil the rice in the chicken stock with bay leaves and salt till almost cooked. Drain the excess stock and set the rice aside .

3 Peel and cut half of the ginger into julienne and make a paste of the rest. Wash and finely chop the green chillies. Wash and chop the coriander and mint leaves. Peel and make a paste of the garlic cloves. Peel and slice the onions and keep aside.

4 Whisk the yogurt. Take half cup of the yogurt and mix two tblspns of coriander leaves and two tblspns of mint leaves. Mix red chilli powder and turmeric powder in the remaining yogurt.

5   Mix the chicken mince, salt, two tblspns coriander leaves, half of the green chillies and chopped ginger. Mix well and refrigerate the mixture for thirty minutes.

6   Make walnut sized balls of the chicken mixture. Melt two tablespoons of ghee and cook the balls in it only to sear the edges. Drain and keep aside.

7   Dissolve saffron in hot milk and keep aside.

8   Heat the remaining ghee in a pan and temper with cumin seeds. Add mace, green cardamom and cloves. Add sliced onions and sauté till golden brown. Add ginger and garlic pastes and remaining chopped green chillies. Mix coriander powder in this. Stir in remaining yogurt with red chilli powder and turmeric powder.

9   Add the chicken balls and one cup of stock and salt. Cook till the gravy is reduced.

10 In a narrow mouthed degchi, first form a layer of half of the chicken koftas, cover it with a layer of half the quantity of cooked rice and sprinkle a little of the yogurt-coriander-mint leaves mixture. Sprinkle half of garam masala powder, ginger julienne and saffron dissolved in hot milk. Continue with these layers till all the chicken masala, rice and yogurt mixture is used up. The final layer should be of rice. Sprinkle garam masala powder, ginger julienne and saffron dissolved in milk over the rice layer. Cover with a moist cloth and seal the degchi with a lid.

11 Cook in a pre-heated oven for fifteen to twenty minutes. Serve hot with raita of your choice.

Chef's Tip: You can cook and serve this biryani in an oven proof dish. If you want, you can finish cooking the biryani in a microwave oven also. In that case cook covered on MICRO HIGH for four minutes only.

GOSHT BIRYANI

INGREDIENTS

Mutton or lamb .... 1 kg	Coriander powder .... 2 tblspns
Basmati rice ....2 cups	Cumin powder .... 1 tblspn
Whole garam masala ....1 tblspn	Red chilli powder .... 1 tspn
Yogurt ....2 cups	Garam masala powder .... 2 tspns
Sliced onions .... 2 cups	Saffron .... a generous pinch
Ghee or oil ....5 tblspns	Warm milk .... ½ cup
Green chillies 2	Ginger ....1 two inch piece
Ginger paste .... 2 tblspns	Fresh coriander leaves ....½ cup
Garlic paste ....2 tblspns	Fresh mint leaves ....½ cup
Chopped tomatoes ....2 cups	Butter ....50 gms
Salt .... as per taste	**For garnishing**
Turmeric powder ....1 tspn	Fried sliced onions

METHOD OF PREPARATION

1 Clean mutton or lamb and cut into one and half inch sized pieces. Pick, clean and wash rice. Soak rice in water. Chop green chillies. Peel ginger and cut into julienne (thin strips). Wash coriander and mint leaves and roughly chop them separately.

2 Soak saffron in warm milk and keep aside. Marinade meat pieces with yogurt, salt, turmeric powder and one tablespoon each of ginger and garlic pastes. Marinade for about four hours in a cool place.

3 Cook rice in salted boiling water along with whole garam masala till rice is almost cooked. Strain and keep the rice warm.

4 Heat ghee or oil in a thick-bottomed pan or pressure cooker. Add sliced onion and chopped green chillies. Cook till onion is light golden brown. Make sure to stir continuously.

92

5   Add remaining ginger and garlic pastes and mix well. Add marinated meat and cook on high flame for seven to eight minutes. Now, add coriander powder, cumin powder and red chilli powder. Mix thoroughly.

6   Stir in three cups of water, bring it to a boil, reduce heat and cook covered till meat pieces are almost cooked. Add chopped tomatoes, salt, one teaspoon garam masala powder and chopped fresh coriander leaves. Cook for fifteen minutes on medium heat, stirring occasionally.

7   In case you are cooking meat in the pressure cooker, add chopped tomatoes, salt, garam masala powder, two cups of water and chopped fresh coriander leaves after adding dry spices. Pressure cook till meat pieces are almost cooked. It normally takes two to three whistles to cook the meat.

8   Ensure that the cooked meat does not have too runny a gravy. If that is the case, cook on high flame to reduce water content.

9   Arrange half the quantity of cooked meat in an oven proof dish and spread half the quantity of cooked rice on top of the meat. Sprinkle a little garam masala powder, half amount each of ginger julienne, saffron dissolved in warm milk and mint leaves. Dot the rice with half the quantity of butter. Place a layer of remaining meat on top of the rice, followed by cooked rice and repeat the earlier process with the remaining quantities of ginger julienne, saffron milk, garam masala powder, mint leaves and butter.

10 Cover it with aluminium foil and cook in a pre-heated oven for fifteen to twenty minutes.

11 Serve garnished with fried sliced onions and mixed vegetable raita.

KHASTA KACHORI

INGREDIENTS

Refined flour .... 2 cups	Asafoetida .... a pinch
Salt .... as per taste	Coriander powder .... 1 tspn
Soda bi-carbonate (baking soda) ..... ¼ tspn	Cumin powder .... ¼ tspn
Oil .... 2 tblspns + to fry	Red chilli powder .... ½ tspn
Water .... ½ cup	Fennel powder .... ¼ tspn
Ginger .... 1 one inch piece	Sugar .... ½ tspn
Green Chillies 2-3	Salt .... as per taste
Split black gram *(urad dal)* .... ¹/₃ cup	Ghee .... 4 tblspns

METHOD OF PREPARATION

1. Sieve the flour, salt and soda bi-carbonate together. Add two tblspns of ghee and rub between your palms to get bread crumb texture.
2. Knead into a soft dough with water. Cover with a moist cloth and set aside.
3. Finely chop ginger and green chillies.
4. Soak the urad dal for an hour. Then coarsely grind using a little water.
5. Heat oil in a kadai. Add chopped ginger, chopped green chillies, asafoetida and all the powdered masalas. Stir well and add ground dal. Cook till all the moisture is almost dried up.
6. Add sugar and salt and mix well. Remove off the flame. Let the mixture cool.
7. Make twelve balls of the flour dough. Flatten each ball between your palms so that they are thinner around the edges and thicker in the centre.
8. Place a little stuffing in the centre and bring the edges together to form a ball. Flatten slightly.
9. Heat oil in a kadai. Fry kachoris on a slow flame till golden brown and crisp.
10. Serve with tamarind chutney.

INGREDIENTS

Rice .... 1 ½ cups	Fenugreek seeds (*methi seeds*) ...½ tspn
Salt .... as per taste	Peanuts .... ½ cup
Oil/ghee ....2 tblspns	Mustard seeds (optional) .... ½ tspn
Asafoetida .... a pinch	Curry leaves 10-12
Dried red chillies 2	Lemon juice .... 3 tblspns
Split black gram (*urad dal*) ..... 1 tblspn	Turmeric powder ....½ tspn
Split gram (*chana dal*) ....1 tblspn	Grated fresh coconut(optional) ..1 tblspn

METHOD OF PREPARATION

1 Pick, wash and soak rice for about thirty minutes. Drain and then boil in plenty of boiling salted water until almost done. Drain and keep aside.

2 Heat oil/ghee in a shallow pan or a kadai. Add a pinch of asafoetida. Add dried red chillies broken into two, urad dal, chana dal and methi seeds. Cook until dals change colour to light brown.

3 Add peanuts and mustard seeds. Let mustard seeds crackle, then add curry leaves. Mix turmeric powder in this. Stir fry for half a minute. Add cooked rice, salt and lemon juice.

4 Garnish with grated coconut.

Chef's Tip: You can use roasted or fried peanuts for this recipe.

LEMON RICE

INGREDIENTS

Refined flour (*maida*) .... 2 cups
Salt .... 1 tspn
Ghee .... 1 tblspn

Water .... 1 cup approximately
Oil .... for deep frying

METHOD OF PREPARATION

1 Sieve flour with salt. Add ghee and make a soft dough with water. Keep covered with a moist cloth for half an hour.

2 Divide into twenty equal parts and make small balls.

3 Roll into 3″ diameter discs.

4 Heat oil in a kadai and fry the luchis till well puffed and cream coloured.

5 Serve hot with dal or any curry of your choice.

INGREDIENTS

Ginger ....2 one inch pieces

Green chillies 4-5

Turmeric powder .... ½ tspn

Corn kernels ....1 cup

Lemon juice ....2 tblspns

Rice .... 1 ¼ cups

Coriander leaves ....2 tblspns

Ghee .... 3 tblspns

Cumin seeds ....1 tspn

Asafoetida ....a pinch

Salt ....as per taste

Water for cooking rice ......3 ½ cups

METHOD OF PREPARATION

1 Peel and chop ginger finely. Wash and chop green chillies and keep aside. Wash and chop the fresh coriander leaves. Wash and soak the rice for half an hour.

2 Boil the corn in water with lemon juice till tender. Drain and keep aside.

3 Heat ghee in a degchi. Add cumin seeds. Once they start to change colour, add asafoetida and then add chopped ginger, chopped green chillies and turmeric powder. Mix well and cook for two or three minutes.

4 Add cooked corn and water and bring to a boil. Add rice and salt, mix and cook on a slow flame till rice is cooked and the khichdi is of the right consistency.

5 Garnish with chopped coriander leaves and serve hot with yogurt, papad and pickle of your choice.

Chef's Tip : Consistency of khichdi is a matter of personal preference. If you want khichdi to be not-too-runny, add a little less water.

97

MAKAI KI KHICHDI

INGREDIENTS

Wheat flour (*atta*) .... 1 cup	Oil .... 4 tblspns
Red chilli powder .... 1 tspn	Chopped fenugreek (*methi*) leaves ....1 cup
Salt .... to taste	Ripe banana .... half
Yogurt .... ½ cup	Gram flour (*besan*) .... ½ cup
Ghee .... 3 tblspns	

METHOD OF PREPARATION

1 Sieve atta, besan along with salt and red chilli powder. Peel and mash banana.

2 Add chopped methi leaves, ghee and yogurt and mix well. Add mashed banana, two tblspns of oil and knead into a stiff dough. Keep covered with a damp cloth and leave it for twenty minutes.

3 Divide into eight equal portions. Roll out each into a 5" diskette.

4 Cook on a hot tawa, applying a little oil till both sides are cooked and lightly golden brown.

Chef's Tip : This dough does not need any water and the parantha can stay fresh for three or four days. It is ideal food on long journies.

98

METHI PARANTHA

MURGH BIRYANI

INGREDIENTS

Rice, basmati	1 ½ cups	Tomatoes	4 medium sized
Chicken pieces	600 gms	Yogurt	1 cup
Whole garam masala	2 tblspns	Saffron	½ gm
Sliced onions	1 cup	Garam masala powder	3 tspns
Chopped ginger	2 tblspns	Milk	½ cup
Chopped garlic	1 tblspn	Butter	50 gms
Red chilli powder	3 tblspns	Golden fried sliced onions	¾ cup
Coriander powder	1 tblspn	Ginger	2 one inch pieces
Turmeric powder	2 tblspns	Oil	3 tblspns
Bay leaves	2	Mint leaves	½ cup
Chopped green coriander	1 tblspn		

METHOD OF PREPARATION

1 Pick, wash and soak rice in water for about thirty minutes.

2 Boil water, add half of the whole garam masala, bay leaves and salt. Drain and add rice, boil till three-fourths done. Drain rice and keep aside.

3 Peel ginger and cut into julienne (thin strips). Wash and chop tomatoes.

4 Mix salt, chopped garlic, yogurt, half of the red chilli powder and half of the chopped ginger. Keep the chicken pieces in this for an hour.

5 Heat oil in a patila or a thick-bottomed pan. Add remaining whole garam masala. Let it crackle. Add sliced onions and sauté until light golden brown.

6 Then add remaining chopped ginger, chopped garlic, coriander powder, turmeric powder, red chilli powder, one tspn garam masala powder and chopped tomatoes. Cook for about five minutes.

7 Add marinated chicken and cook on high heat for five minutes. Simmer for ten to fifteen minutes or till chicken pieces are tender. Add chopped green coriander and mix well.

8 Dissolve saffron in warm milk and keep aside. Now arrange alternate layers of cooked chicken and rice. Sprinkle saffron dissolved in milk, remaining garam masala powder, ginger julienne, mint leaves, golden fried sliced onions and butter in between the layers and on top. Make sure that you end with the rice layers topped with saffron and spices.

9 Cover and seal with aluminium foil or roti dough. Cook in a pre-heated oven, for ten to twelve minutes. Alternatively, cook on an indirect low flame for ten to twelve minutes.

10 Serve hot with raita of your choice.

NAAN

INGREDIENTS

Refined Wheat Flour *(maida)* ...... 4 cups
Milk .... 1 cup
Baking powder .... 1 tspn
Water .... as required
Soda bi-carbonate (baking soda) ... ½ tspn
Oil .... 2 tblspns

Salt .... 1 tspn
Onion seeds .... 2 tspns
Egg 1
Sugar .... 2 tspns
Butter .... 2 tspns
Yogurt .... 2 tblspns

METHOD OF PREPARATION

1 Sieve flour with baking powder, baking soda and salt. Add sugar, egg, milk, yogurt and water. Knead well into a medium soft dough.

2 Apply a little oil and keep it under wet cloth for one hour.

3 Make eight equal portions of the dough. Apply a little oil and put the onion seeds on top.

4 Press sides first and then centre of the dough ball. Give a round flat shape. Pick in hand and pat to give it a round shape of about six inches diameter.

5 Stretch it from one side to give a triangular shape. Put it on a cloth and put it on a pre-heated tandoor wall or cook in a pre-heated oven (200 degrees Celsius).

6 Remove using skewers when it is crisp and brown on both sides.

7 Serve hot, topped with butter.

Chef's Tip : If you don't consume eggs, proceed with this recipe without egg. The loss of taste and texture would hardly be noticeable.

INGREDIENTS

Spinach leaves *(palak)* .... 500 gms
Green chillies 3-4
Whole wheat flour *(atta)* .... 1 ¼ cups

Salt .... as per taste
Ghee .... ½ cup

METHOD OF PREPARATION

1 Clean and wash the palak leaves. Set aside 100 gms and chop them coarsely. Blanch the rest and refresh in cold water.

2 Wash and remove the seeds and roughly chop the green chillies.

3 Puree the blanched palak leaves and green chillies together.

4 Sieve the atta with salt and make a soft dough with palak puree, chopped palak and water if needed. Cover with a moist cloth and keep aside for thirty minutes.

5 Divide into eight equal portions. Roll out each, spread some ghee and fold into half.

6 Fold again into a quarter. Roll out into triangles with each side of 6" approximately.

7 Heat a tawa and place the parantha over it. Turn it and spread some ghee round it. Turn again and spread some ghee on the other side too. Cook till both sides are evenly cooked.

8 Serve hot with yogurt.

PALAK PARANTHA

PUDINA PARANTHA

INGREDIENTS

Whole wheat flour *(atta)* ..... 2 cups

Salt .... 1 tspn

Mint leaves *(pudina)* .... 1 cup

Butter .... 3 tblspns

METHOD OF PREPARATION

1 Sieve whole wheat flour and salt together. Add water to whole wheat flour and salt mixture and knead into a stiff dough. Keep it covered with a wet cloth for twenty to twenty-five minutes.

2 Dry half the mint leaves on a hot tawa, cool and crush to a powder. Chop the remaining mint leaves.

3 Mix the rest of the mint leaves with the dough.

4 Divide the dough into six equal portions. Shape them into balls.

5 Now roll the dough to a medium chappati and smear with butter and sprinkle with flour. Fold the chappati like a fan and twist it back into the form of a ball. Keep aside for five minutes.

6 Roll out each portion into a parantha of 5"-7" diametre and cook on a hot tawa applying a little oil till both sides are lightly golden brown.

7 Sprinkle the dried pudina leaves on the parantha and crush between your palms.

Chef's Tip : If you are cooking Pudina parantha in the tandoor apply a little water on the side that you are going to stick on the tandoor wall.

INGREDIENTS

Basmati rice .... 1 ¾ cups	Green cardamom 4-6
Ginger ....2 one inch pieces	Cloves 4-6
Yogurt ....¾ cup	Large cardamom 3-4
Mint leaves *(pudina)*..........1 ½ cups	Black pepper corns 8-10
Ghee .... 3 tblpsns	Salt ....as per taste
Bay leaves 2	Water for cooking ....3 ¼ cups

METHOD OF PREPARATION

1 Wash and soak the rice in water for half an hour.

2 Peel ginger and grind it into a paste. Whisk yogurt and keep aside.

3 Pluck the pudina leaves. Wash nicely. Reserve a few for garnish and chop the rest.

4 Heat ghee in a thick-bottomed pan. Add bay leaves, green cardamom, large cardamom, cloves and black peppercorns. When they start to crackle, add ginger paste. Mix well and stir in yogurt, and cook for two to three minutes.

5 Add water and bring to a boil. Add salt.

6 Drain and add rice. Bring to a boil. Add chopped mint leaves, mix lightly. Cover the pan and cook on a slow heat for about eight to ten minutes or till rice is completely cooked.

7 Serve hot, garnished with mint leaves.

PUDINA PULAO

INGREDIENTS

Basmati rice .... 1 ½ cups
Onions .... 2 medium sized
Tomatoes 3-4
Cauliflower cut into florets ....¾ cup
Carrots .... 2 small sized
French beans 10-12
Shelled green peas .... ½ cup
Salt .... as per taste

Ghee .... 3 tblspns
Cumin seeds ....1 tspn
Green cardamom 3-4
Large cardamom 3-4
Cinnamon .... 1 one inch stick
Cloves 4-6
Water .... 3 cups

METHOD OF PREPARATION

1 Wash and soak the rice in water for an hour.

2 Peel and slice onions. Wash and chop tomatoes and keep aside.

3 Peel carrots and dice them into half inch cubes. String beans and cut them into half inch sized pieces.

4 Heat ghee in a thick-bottomed pan, add cumin seeds, green cardamom, large cardamom, cinnamon and cloves. Once they start to crackle, add sliced onions and cook till onions become translucent.

5 Add chopped tomatoes and cook till oil can be seen on the sides of the pan. Add salt and three cups of water and bring to a boil. Add carrots and cook for five minutes.

6 Drain excess water from rice and add rice to the pan. Once it starts to boil, add green peas, cauliflower florets, diced beans and salt. Reduce the heat and cover the pan. Cook till rice is completely done.

7 When the rice is cooked, open the pulao, and lightly stir with a spatula so as to ensure that no lumps are formed.

SABZI AUR TAMATAR KA PULAO

Prawn balchao

Chicken makhani

TAMARIND RICE

INGREDIENTS

Rice ....1 ¼ cups	Tamarind pulp .... 3 tblspns
Whole red chillies 6	Asafoetida ....¼ tspn
Mustard seeds .... 1 tspn	Split gram *(chana dal)* ....2 tblspns
Roasted peanuts .... ¼ cup	Sesame seeds (optional) .....3 tblspns
Curry leaves 10-12	Split black gram
Oil...................................3 tblspns	*(urad dal, dhuli)*....................2 tblspns
Ginger ....1 one inch piece	Turmeric ....½ tspn

METHOD OF PREPARATION

1 Wash and soak the rice in water for half an hour.
2 Drain and cook rice in plenty of boiling water. Once the rice is cooked, strain and spread on a plate. Sprinkle a little oil and mix lightly.
3 Keep aside two red chillies for roasting. Chop ginger finely.
4 Heat two tblspns oil and add four dried red chillies, mustard seeds, chana dal, and urad dal. Sauté for two to three minutes till dals have a brown colour. Add turmeric powder, asafoetida, curry leaves, roasted peanuts and chopped ginger. Stir, fry for half a minute.
5 Add tamarind pulp and salt to the above mixture and cook for some time.
6 Dry roast sesame seeds and grind coarsely with two red chillies.
7 Mix in the dry mixture and tamarind mixture to the rice. Mix well and serve.

BASOONDI

INGREDIENTS

Almonds ....½ cup	Milk .... 1 ½ lts
Charoli seeds (chironji)...... 2 tblspns	Sugar ....¾ cup
Pistachio nuts 8-10	Saffron .... a pinch

METHOD OF PREPARATION

1 Soak almonds in warm water to blanch. Remove the skin. Reserve a few for garnish and make a paste of the rest.

2 Slice almonds reserved for garnish and pistachio nuts. Wash and strain chironji.

3 Bring milk to a boil, simmer over low flame till milk coats the back of the spoon. Stir continuously.

4 Stir in almond paste dissolved in half a cup of water or milk and mix well. Add sugar and saffron and cook till sugar gets fully dissolved.

5 Chill and serve garnished with pista, chironji and almonds.

INGREDIENTS

Gram flour (*besan*) ....4 cups	Ghee ....1 cup
Cashewnuts 12-15	Green cardamom powder ....1 tspn
Almonds 12-15	Powdered sugar ....2 cups

METHOD OF PREPARATION

1 Sieve the besan through a fine sieve and set aside.

2 Coarsely grind cashewnuts and almonds and keep aside.

3 Melt ghee in a kadai. Add besan, cook over low heat till besan is well done and gives an aroma. This normally takes about fifteen to twenty minutes. Add cardamom powder, ground cashewnuts and almonds. Stir and take it off the heat.

4 Let it cool for a while. Finally add the powdered sugar and mix well. You may use your hands to mix this.

5 Shape it into walnut sized spherical shape laddoos and store in an airtight container.

Chef's Tip: While serving Besan laddoos that have been kept for a few days in the refrigerator, warm them for fifteen to twenty seconds in the microwave. They will not only become soft but also seem freshly made.

BESAN KE LADDOO

INGREDIENTS

Mawa *(khoya)* .... 2 cups   Cocoa powder .... 3 tblspns

Oil .... 2 tspns   Sugar .... $^1/_3$ cup

METHOD OF PREPARATION

1   Crumble mawa into fine granules. Grease a tray with oil and keep aside.

2   Cook mawa in a thick-bottomed pan, stirring continuously till it is completely melted and has a thick sauce like consistency. Do not colour.

3   Stir in sugar till it is completely dissolved and mawa is cooked.

4   Remove half of this mixture and pour onto the greased tray. For spreading the mawa evenly on the tray, hold it from two sides and rap it on a hard surface two or three times. Let it cool.

5   Keep the remaining half on a slow flame. Add the cocoa powder and mix well.

6   Pour the cocoa mixture over the earlier mixture. Let it cool completely. Cut into pieces and serve coated with silver leaves *(chandi ka vark)*, if desired.

Chef's Tip: Use an aluminium or steel tray for setting the Chocolate burfi as, while cutting, the knife may leave scratches on the surface of the plate used.

CHOCOLATE BURFI

GULAB JAMUN

INGREDIENTS

Mawa (*khoya*) .... 1 ½ cups

Chenna .... ¼ cup

Cooking soda .... ¼ tspn

Flour (*maida*) .... 3 tblspns

Cardamom powder .... ¼ tspn

Ghee/oil .... to deep fry

Sugar .... 2 cups

METHOD OF PREPARATION

1 Grate khoya and mash chenna. Keep aside.

2 Mix the two along with cooking soda, flour, cardamom powder and a little water to make into a soft dough.

3 Divide into sixteen equal portions and shape into balls.

4 Prepare a sugar syrup with equal quantity of water. Clear the syrup by removing the scum, if any.

5 Heat ghee/oil in a kadai. Add the balls and deep fry on low flame till golden in colour.

6 Drain and soak in the sugar syrup for atleast fifteen to twenty minutes before serving.

Chef's Tip : Temperature of the oil should be low or the jamuns will remain un-cooked from inside. You may stuff Gulab jamuns with saffron and pistachio nuts or mishri.

JALEBI

INGREDIENTS

Flour (maida) ....1 ½ cups
Soda bi-carbonate (baking soda)....1 tspn
Sugar ....2 ½ cups

Cardamom powder .... ½ tspn
Ghee .... to deep fry
Yellow or saffron colour (optional) ....a pinch

METHOD OF PREPARATION

1 Mix flour and cooking soda. Add some water and make a smooth batter. Make sure that there are no lumps. Leave it overnight to ferment.

2 Mix it again, add a little water if required and make it into a pouring consistency.

3 Prepare sugar syrup by adding equal quantity of sugar and water. Add cardamom powder and cook it for twenty minutes.

4 Heat ghee in a jalebi tawi or a flat kadai or a frying pan. Pour batter into a jalebi cloth and then pour it into medium hot ghee giving it a jalebi shape. Start from outside to inside for better results.

5 Cook it from both sides till crisp. Remove and keep it in sugar syrup for at least five minutes before serving.

Chef's Tip : For the jalebi cloth, take some cloth and make a three mm hole in the centre. Jalebi making takes some practice and patience. To start with, try making individual jalebis and when you have perfected that, try making them together in a row.
To make crisp jalebis add a little rice flour to maida.

INGREDIENTS

Milk .... 1 ½ lits

Mawa *(khoya)* .... 50 gms

Green cardamom 3

Flour *(maida)* .... 3 tblspns

For the Sugar syrup

Water .... 2 cups

Natural yellow colour (optional) ...... ¼ tspn

Sugar .... 2 cups

For Garnishing

Pistachio, chopped 15-20

Saffron .... a few strands

METHOD OF PREPARATION

1 Boil milk in a thick heavy-bottomed pan, reduce heat and simmer till it is reduced and reaches a coating consistency. Add grated khoya, and mix well. Bring it to room temperature.

2 Reserve two tblspns of sugar and form a one string sugar syrup with the rest of the sugar.

3 Dissolve saffron in two tblspns of hot milk. Add it to the sugar syrup.

4 Add flour and the reserved sugar to the reduced milk. Mix well and make a batter of pouring consistency using a little milk if required.

5 Heat ghee in a wide mouthed flat bottomed kadai. Pour a ladle full of batter to form a small pancake. Cook on slow to medium heat.

6 Turn it over when it starts to colour slightly. When both sides are done, drain and immerse in the sugar syrup.

7 Sprinkle a little of the chopped pistachio and saffron. Serve hot.

Chef's Tip : Serve hot Malpuas with chilled rabdi, it tastes divine.

MALPUA

MATAR KI KHEER

INGREDIENTS

Shelled green peas ....1 cup
Ghee ....½ cup
Milk ....1 ¼ litres
Sugar ....1 cup

Green cardamom powder ....1 tspn
Pistachio nuts 20-25
Raisins 20-25

METHOD OF PREPARATION

1 Boil green peas for five minutes. Refresh in cold water and grind to a fine paste.

2 Heat ghee in a thick-bottomed pan, add green peas paste and cook for a few minutes, stirring constantly. Keep aside.

3 Boil milk and add it to the cooked green peas paste. Bring it to a boil. Cook on a slow flame for fifteen to twenty minutes or till the milk is reduced to half.

4 Add sugar, green cardamom powder, raisins and sliced pistachio nuts. Cook for about eight to ten minutes on a slow flame, stirring continuously. Serve chilled.

Chef's Tip : When you serve Matar ki kheer, initially serve it as Pista kheer, as most people are not very receptive to the idea of eating kheer made out of green peas. However disclose it later to prompt people to try a second helping.

INGREDIENTS

Gram flour *(besan)*	.................2 cups	Sugar	.... 1 cup
Almonds	8-10	Cardamom powder	.............¼ tspn
Pistachio nuts	 8-10	Nutmeg *(jaiphal)* powder	....¼ tspn
Ghee	..................2 tblspns + ½ cup	Milk	.... 4 tblspns

METHOD OF PREPARATION

1 Sieve the besan and discard the residue.

2 Slice almonds and pistachio nuts and set aside.

3 Heat two tblspns of ghee and four tblspns of milk. Pour this over the besan.

4 Mix thoroughly with your fingers so that no lumps are formed and it resembles bread crumbs. Pass it through a sieve again and set aside.

5 Make a sugar syrup with one cup sugar and three-fourth cup of water. Stir the sugar and water and then heat. The syrup should be a little more than one string consistency. Once ready, keep it aside.

6 Grease a thali and keep aside.

7 Heat half cup ghee in a kadai. Add the treated besan and cook on a low flame till it gives out an aroma and besan turns golden brown. Stir constantly.

8 Add cardamom powder and nutmeg powder. Remove from the flame and add the hot sugar syrup when the besan mixture is still hot. Mix continuously to ensure that no lumps are formed. Continue to mix till it reaches setting consistency.

9 Pour onto the greased thali and rap it on a flat surface to flatten it. Garnish with sliced almonds and pistachio nuts. Let it cool and set.

10 Cut into the required shape and serve.

MOHAN THAL

MOONG DAL HALWA

INGREDIENTS

Split green gram, skinless (moong dal, dhuli) .... 1 cup	Milk .... ½ cup
Sugar .... 1 cup	Mawa (khoya) .... ¾ cup
Saffron .... a generous pinch	Ghee .... 1 cup
	Almonds 10-12

METHOD OF PREPARATION

1 Wash and soak the moong dal for six hours. Grind coarsely using very little water.

2 Prepare one string sugar syrup with the sugar and one and half cups of water.

3 Soak saffron in hot milk. Crumble mawa into fine granules. Blanch almonds in boiling hot water for five minutes. Cool and peel them, cut them into thin slivers.

4 Heat ghee in a thick-bottomed pan and add the ground moong dal. Keep stirring over a low flame till the dal turns golden brown. This needs time and patience. Do not rush through this step.

5 Add the sugar syrup and saffron milk, stir till they are thoroughly incorporated and the halwa is of dropping consistency. Add mawa and cook till it dissolves.

6 Serve hot, garnished with sliced almonds.

Chef's Tip: Add one tblspn besan to melted ghee before putting the ground moong dal. It helps in even cooking of ground moong dal and also avoids lump formation during cooking.

INGREDIENTS

Rice ....5 tblspns	Pistachio nuts 10-15
Saffron ....a generous pinch	Sugar ....¾ cup
Milk .... 1 lt	Green cardamom powder ....½ tspn

METHOD OF PREPARATION

1 Pick, wash and soak rice for half an hour and then grind it to a coarse paste.

2 Blanch pistachio nuts in hot water, cool, remove skin and slice.

3 Bring milk to a boil. Add rice paste dissolved in a little water or cold milk. Cook till rice is completely cooked. Stir constantly. Add saffron and mix well.

4 Add sugar, cardamom powder and cook till sugar is completely dissolved.

5 Pour into earthenware or china bowls and garnish with sliced pista.

6 Chill in a refrigerator for an hour before serving.

Chef's Tip : It is a good idea to grind green cardamom with a little sugar as otherwise the quantity of green cardamom may be too little to grind. You can store this in an airtight jar for use in sweet dishes and desserts.

PHIRNI

RASMALAI

INGREDIENTS

Chenna .... 250 gms

Pistachio nuts 10-12

Refined flour (maida) ....4 tblspns

Sugar ....4 cups

Milk ....2 lts

METHOD OF PREPARATION

1 Crumble the chenna and mash it. Add two tblspns maida and mash again with the palm of your hand to make a dough.

2 Divide into sixteen equal portions, roll into balls and press slightly to flatten them.

3 Blanch pistachio nuts in hot water, cool, remove skin and slice.

4 Dissolve two cups of sugar in the same quantity of water, bring to a boil, add the rest of the flour dissolved in a little water.

5 Slowly lower the chenna balls in the boiling syrup and cook over high flame for ten minutes. Add half a cup of water and bring to a boil again. Cook for three minutes.

6 Meanwhile prepare a thin sugar syrup with one cup sugar and two cups of water.

7 Soak the cooked chenna balls in this syrup.

8 Boil the milk in a thick-bottomed pan, lower the flame and continue to boil till it is reduced to a thick consistency. Stir continuously.

9 Add the rest of the sugar to reduced milk and keep boiling till the sugar is dissolved. Take it off the fire, cool and refrigerate for an hour.

10 Squeeze the chenna balls and put them into the chilled and sweetened reduced milk. Refrigerate it for another half an hour.

11 Serve chilled, garnished with sliced pistachio.

Chef's Tip : Use chenna made from cow's milk. Best chenna is made by curdling cow's milk with leftover whey of chenna made earlier. The trick lies in curdling and the acid content should be just right, if it is too much, the chenna would become tough.

GLOSSARY

English	Hindi	
Ingredients		
Almond	Badam	Used as a garnish for sweets and as an ingredient in pulaos and curries.
Asafoetida	Hing	A powerful seasoning, used to flavour curries.
Bay leaves	Tej patta	These dried leaves are used to flavour curries and rice.
Black cardamom	Badi ilaichi	Used for flavouring curries and pulaos.
Black gram	Urad (whole)	The split form, urad dal and whole urad is used to make curries.
Black peppercorn	Kali mirch	This hot, pungent spice is an important ingredient in hot garam masala. The pepper powder is often used in curries, rice and savoury dishes.
Capsicum	Simla mirch	Used as a vegetable and also in salads.
Caraway	Shah jeera	Used for flavouring curries and pulaos.
Carom seeds	Ajwain	Also known as Bishop's weed. Used as a part of batters, masalas and in savoury dishes.
Cashewnuts	Kaju	Used in sweets and pulao as a garnish and cashew paste is used to flavour and thicken curries.
Chick peas	Kabuli Chana, chole	Split chick peas - chana dal is used to make curries.
Chilli	Mirch	Green or dried red chillies or red chilli powder are used extensively in Indian cooking to make the food hot.
Cinnamon	Dalchini	These dry sticks are used to flavour curries and rice and is an ingredient in garam masala.
Clove	Laung	Used in both sweet and savoury dishes.
Coconut	Narial	An important part of South Indian cooking. The milk and flesh extracted from the coconut is used as a base for curries, soups, chutneys and sweets.
Coriander seeds	Dhania	Used whole and in the powdered form in curries and vegetables and as a part of garam masala.

117

Cottage cheese (Indian)	Paneer	Used in vegetables as well as a base in sweet dishes.
Cumin seeds	Jeera	Used whole or ground, it imparts a spicy, aromatic flavour to curries, pulaos and raitas. Light roasting in a dry pan enhances the aroma.
Curry leaves	Kadhi patta	Used fresh or dried, they have a warm, appetizing aroma and give a delicate, spicy flavour to the dish. Used extensively in South Indian cooking.
Dry mango powder	Amchur	Used in curries and vegetables to give sour and tangy taste.
Fennel	Saunf	These dried seeds used extensively to flavour curries and pickles, have a sweet aromatic flavour.
Fenugreek leaves	Methi	Fresh leaves are used as a vegetable and in paranthas. Dried leaves known as kasoori methi are used for seasoning curries.
Fenugreek seeds	Methi dana	Whole seeds are used for seasoning, whereas the powder is an essential ingredient of pickles. For best results, lightly roast.
Fresh cream	Malai	Used in sweets and some curries. Home-made malai can be obtained by letting boiled milk cool and skimming off the layer of fat that forms on the surface.
Garlic	Lehsoon	Often used whole or as paste, in combination with ginger to flavour curries and pulaos.
Ginger	Adrak	Used as fresh or in the paste form in curries and vegetables. Dried ginger root is sometimes used to flavour pickles.
Ginger powder	Saunth	This can be used in place of fresh ginger. Popular in Kashmiri food.
Gramflour	Besan	Ground gram/chana dal, used in many sweet and savoury dishes.
Green cardamom	Chhoti ilaichi	Used whole, as a part of garam masala and in the powdered form to flavour sweets and some rice dishes.

Green coriander	Hara dhania	Used in curries and vegetables as well as for garnishing.
Green gram	Moong	Used as whole, bean sprouts or split -- as dal. Skinless split gram (moong, dhuli) is used for making curries and halwa.
Green peas	Matar	These can be used fresh or frozen.
Honey	Shahad	Used as a sugar substitute.
Jaggery	Gud	A sugar substitute, imparts a delicate earthy taste to the dish.
Mace	Javantri/javitri	It is the outer covering of nutmeg. It has a delicate flavour and is used as an ingredient in masalas.
Mint	Pudina	These leaves are widely used in chutneys and as a flavouring for yogurt and in appetizers. Dried leaves are ground to make mint powder.
Mustard seeds	Rai/sarson	Whole seeds are used for tempering and as powder, in pickles.
Nutmeg	Jaiphal	The sweet-woody scent gives a special flavour to sweet dishes.
Okra (Lady's fingers)	Bhindi	Used as a vegetable.
Onion	Piaz	Chopped and as paste, it is used as a base in many curries and vegetables. Different gravies require different onion pastes. For instance, white gravies require boiled onion paste while red gravies use brown onion paste.
Onion seeds	Kalonji	Dry onion seeds are used in pickles and as a topping for Naans.
Pigeon peas	Toor	These in their split form are used to make curries.
Poppy seeds	Khus khus	Used to thicken curries.
Refined flour	Maida	Used as a base to make different Indian breads and also to make snacks.

Rose water	Gulab jal	Rose water and rose essence are especially used in Indian sweets like Gulab jamoons and in sherbets.
Saffron	Kesar	This rare and expensive spice is used in minute quantities to flavour milk-based sweets and sometimes in special curries and biryanis. To get maximum flavour, saffron should be dissolved in warm milk for about twenty minutes before use.
Semolina	Rawa	Used to make Indian breads like paranthas, puris and as a base in some sweets.
Sesame seeds	Til	The seeds are used in some sweets. Sesame paste is sometimes added to flavour and thicken the spicy curries. Sesame oil is used for cooking in some parts of the country. For better flavour, slightly roast the seeds until they jump.
Soda bi-carbonate	Baking soda	Used for raising the flour.
Star anise	Badiyan/Phoolchakri	This dried, reddish-brown fruit, used in small quantities, gives a distinctive aroma to the dish.
Sweet potato	Rataloo (Shakarkand)	This has a sweetish taste and can be fried, boiled, roasted or cooked in a gravy.
Tamarind	Imli	Added to curries to give a mild refreshing sour taste. Tamarind pulp, which can be stored in the refrigerator, is used more often in curries and chutneys. When combined with sugar and other spices, mixed with cold water, it makes a delightful cooling drink.
Turmeric	Haldi	The yellow-coloured powder of the turmeric root gives a distinct flavour and colour to the curries, vegetables and pulaos. It also has medicinal properties.
Wheat flour	Atta	Whole meal flour is used as a base to make different Indian breads.
Yogurt/Curd	Dahi	Yogurt is added to cooked dishes and also as a base for raitas, snacks like Dahi vadas and consumed in its liquid form as lassi or buttermilk.

Some Indian terms

Charoli seeds	Also known as Chironji. Used as garnish in sweets.
Chenna	A form of cottage cheese, used as a base for sweets like Rasagoola or rasmalai.
Garam masala	Spice powder. Lightly roast and grind the following ingredients to make the masala: Black cardamom 8-10; Green cardamom 15-20; Cinnamon 15-20 pieces (1" each); Cloves 1 tblspn; Mace 1 flower; Nutmeg 1; Peppercorn 1 tblspn; Cumin seeds 1/2 cup; Coriander seeds 2 tblspns.
Ghee	Clarified butter. Used as a cooking medium in some dishes instead of oil.
Goda masala	A spice powder, also called 'sweet mix', containing most of the ingredients from the garam masala, with extra Cumin seeds and whole dried red chillies.
Kokum	This sour, dry red fruit, also known as amsool or red mango is used in some curries for its sour flavour.
Masala	Spice powders. Indian cooking uses different kinds of masalas such as Garam masala, goda masala, chaat masala.
Mawa	Khoya. Used as a base for sweets and as a thickener in some curries.

Some Indian utensils

Degchi	A wide, thick-bottomed vessel.
Handi	A heavy-bottomed vessel, used to cook vegetables, curries, rice.
Kadai	A deep pan, mainly used for deep-frying.

Katori	A small bowl.
Patila	A large bowl, a thin-bottomed vessel.
Tandoor	A traditional clay oven fired by charcoal. Used for baking breads like Naan and Tandoori roti and for roasting meat, vegetables and paneer. The charcoal fire gives a smoked flavour to the dish.
Tawa	A thick, flat pan, used to make Indian breads like rotis, paranthas.
Tawi	A shallow frying pan, used for jalebis.
Thali	A metal plate.

Some cooking methods

Baste	Moisten with gravy or melted fat/butter during cooking.
Blanch	Immerse briefly in boiling water.
Broil	Roast/Lightly fry. Also a term used for cooking meat.
Deep frying	Fry in a lot of oil/ghee
Marinate	Soak meat, fish etc., before cooking, in a mixture of oil, spices, and for a few recipes, yogurt.
Puree	Make a soft pulp of vegetables or fruit and reduce to a smooth paste.
Roast	Heat/lightly fry, before grinding in cases of spices. Cook in an oven.
Sauté	Quickly fry in a little hot oil.
Temper	(Tadka, baghar) The first step in certain recipes: Heat oil. Add mustard seeds/cumin seeds to it. After they crackle, add the other spices/curry leaves.

Subscribe to www.sanjeevkapoor.com NOW

Subscribe now, get fabulous discounts! Have the benefit of saving and also enjoy free books!!

Access to more than 1000 recipes besides many other sections, which will be a rare culinary treat to any food lover. In addition to online contests, etc., you will also have opportunities to win fabulous prizes.

Sanjeev Kapoor also invites all food lovers to participate in the Khana Khazana quiz and win BIG prizes every week. Watch Khana Khazana on Zee TV, answer correctly, one simple question based on that day's episode, combine it with a favourite recipe of yours and you can be the lucky winner going places!

Type	One year Subscription to www.sanjeevkapoor.com	Sanjeev Kapoor's 3 Best Selling Books Absolutely free	Total worth	You pay (offer value)	You Save	Your Choice
Yellow Chilli	Rs.1000/-	Rs.750*	Rs.1750/-	Rs.750/- (US $ 13)+	Rs.1000/-	☐
Red Chilli	Rs.1000/-	....	Rs.1000/-	Rs.500/- (US $ 10)+	Rs.500/-	☐

* Conditions Apply

*   For subscribers requesting delivery of the free books within India an additional sum of Rs.50 (Rupees Fifty only) will be levied as delivery charges.
*   For subscribers requesting delivery outside India, additional Rs.500/- delivery charges will be levied for airmail charges on the Yellow Chilli offer.
+   Foreign exchange rates are approximate.

HURRY!!! OFFER OPEN TO FIRST 1000 SUBSCRIBERS ONLY
Choose your three free books with the Yellow Chilli subscription

Khazana of Indian Recipes	Khazana of Healthy Tasty Recipes	Khana Khazana — Celebration of Indian Cooking	Low Calorie Vegetarian Cookbook	Any Time Temptations	Best of Chinese Cooking	Microwave Cooking Made Easy	Simply Indian
MRP: Rs 250	MRP: Rs 250	MRP: Rs 250	MRP: Rs 250	MRP: Rs 225	MRP: Rs 250	MRP: Rs 250	MRP: Rs 250
☐	☐	☐	☐	☐	☐	☐	☐

I'm enclosing Cheque/DD No. _____ dated _____ for

Rs._____ (in words) _____ on

(specify bank and branch) _____

favouring Popular Prakashan Pvt Ltd, Mumbai

For Credit Cards

Charge Card ☐ VISA ☐ Master Card for Rs. _____

Credit Card No. ☐☐☐☐☐☐☐☐☐☐☐☐☐☐☐☐

Card Expiry Date ☐☐ ☐☐ Card Member's Date Birth ☐☐ ☐☐ ☐☐☐☐

              MM YY   DD MM YYYY

Card Member's Name _____

For ☐ Yellow Chilli Subscription ☐ Red Chilli Subscription

Name: Mr./Ms _____

Address: _____

_____

City: _____ Pin: _____ State: _____

Country: _____ Phone Res.: _____

Off.: _____ E-mail: _____

Please fill in the coupon in capital letters and mail it with your Cheque/DD to :

Popular Prakashan Pvt Ltd,
35-C, Pt. Madan Mohan Malaviya Marg,
Tardeo, Mumbai - 400 034.
Phone   : 022-24941656, 24944295
Fax   : 022-24945294
E-mail : info@popularprakashan.com
Website : www.popularprakashan.com

*Delivery subject to realisation of Cheque/DD.
Please allow two weeks for processing your subscription. Please superscribe your name and address on the reverse of the Cheque/DD.
All disputes are subject to the exclusive jurisdiction of competent courts and forums in Mumbai (India) only.

This Voucher entitles the bearer redemption of Rs.50/- against purchase of Sanjeev Kapoor's books worth minimum Rs.100/-

Valid upto 31st December 2005

This Voucher entitles the bearer redemption of Rs.50/- against purchase of Sanjeev Kapoor's books worth minimum Rs.100/-

Valid upto 31st December 2005

This Voucher entitles the bearer redemption of Rs.100/- against purchase of Sanjeev Kapoor's books worth minimum Rs.300/-

Valid upto 31st December 2005

This Voucher entitles the bearer redemption of Rs.100/- against purchase of Sanjeev Kapoor's books worth minimum Rs.300/-

Valid upto 31st December 2005

For further enquiries contact:

Popular Prakashan Pvt. Ltd.
35-C, Pt. Madan Mohan Malaviya Marg, Tardeo, Mumbai-400 034
Phone: 91-22-24941656 Fax: 91-22-24945294
E-Mail: info@popularprakashan.com
Website: www.popularprakashan.com, www.sanjeevkapoor.com

TERMS AND CONDITIONS FOR REDEMPTION

1. This coupon can be redeemed against the purchase of Sanjeev Kapoor books by sending this coupon along with payment to Popular Prakashan.
2. The offer is valid as per the mentioned date.
3. The coupons are valid only against the printed MRPs and will not work with any other special offers or promotions at the time of purchase.
4. The coupons are non-transferable and non-encashable.
5. No two vouchers can be clubbed together.
6. Each coupon is valid for one time purchase only.

Popular Prakashan Pvt. Ltd.
35-C, Pt. Madan Mohan Malaviya Marg, Tardeo, Mumbai-400 034
E-Mail: info@popularprakashan.com
Phone: 91-22-24941656 Fax: 91-22-24945294

TERMS AND CONDITIONS FOR REDEMPTION

1. This coupon can be redeemed against the purchase of Sanjeev Kapoor books by sending this coupon along with payment to Popular Prakashan.
2. The offer is valid as per the mentioned date.
3. The coupons are valid only against the printed MRPs and will not work with any other special offers or promotions at the time of purchase.
4. The coupons are non-transferable and non-encashable
5. No two vouchers can be clubbed together.
6. Each coupon is valid for one time purchase only.

Popular Prakashan Pvt. Ltd.
35-C, Pt. Madan Mohan Malaviya Marg, Tardeo, Mumbai-400 034
E-Mail: info@popularprakashan.com
Phone: 91-22-24941656 Fax: 91-22-24945294

TERMS AND CONDITIONS FOR REDEMPTION

1. This coupon can be redeemed against the purchase of Sanjeev Kapoor books by sending this coupon along with payment to Popular Prakashan.
2. The offer is valid as per the mentioned date.
3. The coupons are valid only against the printed MRPs and will not work with any other special offers or promotions at the time of purchase.
4. The coupons are non-transferable and non-encashable.
5. No two vouchers can be clubbed together.
6. Each coupon is valid for one time purchase only.

Popular Prakashan Pvt. Ltd.
35-C, Pt. Madan Mohan Malaviya Marg, Tardeo, Mumbai-400 034
E-Mail: info@popularprakashan.com
Phone: 91-22-24941656 Fax: 91-22-24945294

TERMS AND CONDITIONS FOR REDEMPTION

1. This coupon can be redeemed against the purchase of Sanjeev Kapoor books by sending this coupon along with payment to Popular Prakashan.
2. The offer is valid as per the mentioned date.
3. The coupons are valid only against the printed MRPs and will not work with any other special offers or promotions at the time of purchase.
4. The coupons are non-transferable and non-encashable.
5. No two vouchers can be clubbed together.
6. Each coupon is valid for one time purchase only.

Popular Prakashan Pvt. Ltd.
35-C, Pt. Madan Mohan Malaviya Marg, Tardeo, Mumbai-400 034
E-Mail: info@popularprakashan.com
Phone: 91-22-24941656 Fax: 91-22-24945294